GUID

GW00689743

1
20

Edited by **Helen Paynter** and **David Spriggs**

The Bible Reading Fellowship
15 The Chambers, Vineyard
Abingdon OX14 3FE
brf.org.uk

The Bible Reading Fellowship (BRF) is a Registered Charity (233280)

ISBN 978 0 85746 900 7
All rights reserved

This edition © The Bible Reading Fellowship 2019
Cover image © iStock.com/LoraSi

Distributed in Australia by:
MediaCom Education Inc, PO Box 610, Unley, SA 5061
Tel: 1 800 811 311 | admin@mediacom.org.au

Distributed in New Zealand by:
Scripture Union Wholesale, PO Box 760, Wellington
Tel: 04 385 0421 | suwholesale@clear.net.nz

Acknowledgements
Scripture quotations from The New Revised Standard Version of the Bible, Anglicised
edition (NSRV), are copyright © 1989, 1995 by the Division of Christian Education of
the National Council of the Churches of Christ in the United States of America. Used by
permission. All rights reserved.

Scripture quotations taken from the Holy Bible, English Standard Version (ESV), are
published by HarperCollins Publishers, © 2001 Crossway Bibles, a division of Good
News Publishers. Used by permission. All rights reserved.

Scripture quotations taken from The Message are copyright © 1993, 1994, 1995, 1996,
2000, 2001, 2002 by Eugene H. Peterson. Used by permission of NavPress. All rights
reserved. Represented by Tyndale House Publishers, Inc.

Scripture quotations taken from the New American Standard Bible® (NASB) are
copyright © 1960, 1962, 1963, 1968, 1971, 1972, 1973, 1975, 1977, 1995 by The
Lockman Foundation. Used by permission. (www.Lockman.org)

Extracts from the Authorised Version of the Bible (The King James Bible, KJV), the
rights in which are vested in the Crown, are reproduced by permission of the Crown's
Patentee, Cambridge University Press.

Every effort has been made to trace and contact copyright owners for material used
in this resource. We apologise for any inadvertent omissions or errors, and would
ask those concerned to contact us so that full acknowledgement can be made in
the future.

A catalogue record for this book is available from the British Library

Printed by Gutenberg Press, Tarxien, Malta

Suggestions for using *Guidelines*

Set aside a regular time and place, if possible, when and where you can read and pray undisturbed. Before you begin, take time to be still and, if you find it helpful, use the BRF Prayer on page 6.

In *Guidelines*, the introductory section provides context for the passages or themes to be studied, while the units of comment can be used daily, weekly or whatever best fits your timetable. You will need a Bible (more than one if you want to compare different translations) as Bible passages are not included. Please don't be tempted to skip the Bible reading because you know the passage well. We will have utterly failed if we don't bring our readers into engagement with the word of God. At the end of each week is a 'Guidelines' section, offering further thoughts about or practical application of what you have been studying.

Occasionally, you may read something in *Guidelines* that you find particularly challenging, even uncomfortable. This is inevitable in a series of notes which draws on a wide spectrum of contributors and doesn't believe in ducking difficult issues. Indeed, we believe that *Guidelines* readers much prefer thought-provoking material to a bland diet that only confirms what they already think.

If you do disagree with a contributor, you may find it helpful to go through these three steps. First, think about why you feel uncomfortable. Perhaps this is an idea that is new to you, or you are not happy about the way something has been expressed. Or there may be something more substantial – you may feel that the writer is guilty of sweeping generalisation, factual error, or theological or ethical misjudgement. Second, pray that God would use this disagreement to teach you more about his word and about yourself. Third, have a deeper read about the issue. There are further reading suggestions at the end of each writer's block of notes. And then, do feel free to write to the contributor or the editor of *Guidelines*. We welcome communication, by email, phone or letter, as it enables us to discover what has been useful, challenging or infuriating for our readers. We don't always promise to change things, but we will always listen and think about your ideas, complaints or suggestions. Thank you!

To send feedback, please email **enquiries@brf.org.uk**, phone **+44 (0)1865 319700** or write to the address shown opposite.

Writers in this issue

Steve Hollinghurst is an Anglican priest who works for the Methodist Church national team as Contemporary Apologetics Officer. He is the author of *Mission-Shaped Evangelism* (Canterbury Press, 2010), and he writes and speaks widely on mission and culture.

Helen Morris is a lecturer in applied theology at Moorlands College and is the course leader for the College's BA programmes. She is a ministry leader with Richmond Holidays, where she gets to combine two of her biggest passions: teaching the Bible and skiing.

Bill Goodman encourages and enables lifelong learning among church leaders in the Anglican Diocese of Sheffield. He has enjoyed helping people meet with God as they wrestle with the Bible in various theological courses and colleges, in the UK and overseas.

Ernest Lucas has doctorates in both science and biblical studies. After doing biochemical research, he was a Baptist minister and then vice-principal and tutor in biblical studies at Bristol Baptist College.

Helen Paynter is a Baptist minister, director of the Centre for the Study of Bible and Violence at Bristol Baptist College, and editor of BRF's *Guidelines* Bible reading notes.

Andy Angel is the vicar of St Andrew's, Burgess Hill. Previously, he taught New Testament in Anglican training colleges. He has written various books, including *Playing with Dragons: Living with suffering and God* (Cascade, 2014) and *Intimate Jesus: The sexuality of God incarnate* (SPCK, 2017).

David Spriggs provides occasional consultancy services for Bible Society, but his main role is as a Baptist minister again. He is a part-time minister with the Friar Lane and Braunstone Baptist Church, Leicester.

Nigel G. Wright is a Baptist minister, principal emeritus of Spurgeon's College and a former president of the Baptist Union of Great Britain.

Graham Dow was bishop of Carlisle for eight years, bishop of Willesden (London) and vicar of Holy Trinity Church (Coventry) for eleven years. He loves expounding the Bible, supporting Holy Spirit renewal and praying for healing, the liberation of lay ministry and God's purpose in daily work.

Pauline Hoggarth was born in Peru and served with Scripture Union in three different roles in the UK and overseas. She is the author of *The Seed and the Soil: Engaging with the word of God* (Langham, 2011).

Helen Paynter writes…

Happy new year! Type '2020 the year of…' into an internet search engine, and an interesting set of search terms will be offered. The Catholic Church in Pakistan has designated 2020 the Year of Youth. The World Health Organisation has named 2020 the Year of the Nurse. The United Nations has called 2020 the 'Year of Plant Health', in response to growing anxieties about food security globally.

We will all be beginning the new year with our own personal set of excitements, priorities and concerns. Some will be eagerly anticipating a new life event such as a marriage, retirement, the birth of a child or grandchild. Others will be feeling fear or dread at what the year may bring: in the face of serious illness, impending redundancy, or other major challenges.

But a new year provides an opportunity to stop and reappraise our priorities, our life choices, and our values. And of course for us who acknowledge the lordship of Christ, this reappraisal should involve a spiritual stocktake. Where are we acting in line with the ethical norms of the kingdom of God, and where are we falling short? Where are we responding to the call of God on our lives, and where are we being disobedient? What do we need to press into, and what do we need to repent of? And because we live in a changing world, even if we have not changed, the relationship between our faith and the rest of our lives may have shifted. What are the new things that the Spirit is whispering over us in this season?

My predecessor, David Spriggs, commissioned many of the notes for *Guidelines* this year with this in mind. He invites us to use the beginning of this new year, this new decade, to take a close look at our habits, our practices and our beliefs – as individuals and as church. Are there areas that are slipping, where we need to pay attention? Are there places where our praxis needs to be updated to reflect the changing environment, notwithstanding our belief in the unchanging truths of Christ?

To keep us attentive to these questions, David has used the optometrist's idea of 20:20 vision as a metaphor for our careful examination of ancient beliefs and practices in the year 2020. So, in this edition of *Guidelines*, we have the first of these: Mission and Evangelism 20:20 by Steve Hollinghurst. In later editions this year we will apply the same lens to discipleship, church, reading the Bible, and so on.

We also have some wonderfully inspiring and challenging reflections for Lent and Easter, from David Spriggs, Nigel Wright and Graham Dow. We will be diving deeply into Ephesians, Proverbs, Ezekiel, Matthew and Jeremiah. May God guide and inspire us all as we read, pray, work and seek to hear the words that the Spirit is whispering over us in 2020.

The BRF Prayer

Almighty God,
you have taught us that your word is a lamp for our feet
and a light for our path. Help us, and all who prayerfully
read your word, to deepen our fellowship with you
and with each other through your love.
And in so doing may we come to know you more fully,
love you more truly, and follow more faithfully
in the steps of your son Jesus Christ, who lives and reigns
with you and the Holy Spirit, one God forevermore.
Amen

We want to hear from you!

Complete our short survey for the chance to win a FREE subscription!
Let us know what you like about BRF's Bible reading notes
and how we can improve them to help more people
encounter God through the Bible.

Go to brfonline.org.uk/BRNSURVEY

Mission and evangelism 20:20

Steve Hollinghurst

One of the main debates in 20th-century missiology was the relationship between evangelism and social action. Following the World Wars, churches were divided between those who saw evangelism as the priority and those who prioritised social action. In the late 20th and early 21st century, this dichotomy has mostly disappeared. There is now a new emphasis on what has been called 'holistic' or 'integral mission' among evangelicals and on the importance of evangelism among groups like the World Council of Churches and the Roman Catholic Church. This enabled the production of a landmark document 'Christian witness in a multi-religious world' in 2011, published jointly by the Pontifical Council for Interreligious Dialogue, the World Council of Churches and the World Evangelical Alliance. The idea of such a joint statement on mission and evangelism would have been unheard of 20 years earlier. This is also expressed by other documents, such as the Micah Challenge and the Anglican 'Five Marks of Mission'. Links to these can be found in the reading at the end. The five marks are:

1 To proclaim the good news of the kingdom;
2 To teach, baptise and nurture new believers;
3 To respond to human need by loving service;
4 To seek to transform unjust structures of society, to challenge violence of every kind and to pursue peace and reconciliation;
5 To strive to safeguard the integrity of creation and sustain and renew the life of the earth.

While this document is Anglican, its ethos is that of the wider embrace of integral mission. This week's studies explore that ethos from the perspective of a number of New Testament passages. These examine the relationship of integral mission and evangelism and raise questions for us about how we view our calling as a missionary church.

Unless otherwise stated, Bible quotations are from the New Revised Standard Version (Anglicised).

1 Jesus the Messiah and integral mission

Luke 4:14–30

Luke's account of Jesus reading from Isaiah 61 is like a manifesto for Jesus' ministry. The text of Isaiah Luke cites is closer to the Greek Old Testament, the Septuagint, than the later Hebrew Masoretic text used in Jewish and Christian Bibles. The Masoretic text is part of a prophecy of the return of Israel from exile. Luke's text introduces good news for the poor and healing of the blind not found in the current Hebrew text. Luke is applying the text to Jesus' ministry. Indeed, in Luke 7:20–22 Jesus cites such elements of his ministry as proof to be given to John the Baptist that Jesus is the 'one to come'.

Jesus' hearers at Nazareth marvel at Jesus' words, then turn against him, demanding miraculous proof of what they see as the doubtful claim of a local boy. In this, they echo the devil's tempting of Jesus just before this passage. Jesus' miracles are demonstrations of the kingdom; they are not tricks to prove his identity.

By the time of Jesus, some viewed Isaiah 61 as a yet-to-be-fulfilled messianic prophecy. An example is the Dead Sea Scroll 11Q Melchizedek, in which Isaiah 61 is applied to Melchizedek as a coming Messiah. Indeed, the writer to the Hebrews would later develop a parallel between Jesus and Melchizedek, possibly drawing on such a source. What that Dead Sea Scroll also highlights is the relationship between 'the year of the Lord's favour' and the year of Jubilee. The Jubilee was a year when poverty was addressed through the redistribution of land, debts being cancelled and slaves being set free. Jesus' application of the prophecy in Isaiah to himself might therefore indicate his ministry was also about social transformation on the scale of a Jubilee year.

Latin American theologian Gustavo Gutierrez speaks of the gospel addressing three kinds of liberation: social liberation from injustice, personal liberation to enable people to flourish and spiritual liberation from the power of sin. All of these are contained in Jesus' 'Isaiah manifesto', which offers a holistic vision of salvation. This is not a gospel that is about either social transformation or individual salvation, but one in which the two are integral to the kingdom Jesus proclaimed and witnessed to in his ministry.

This is why Jesus continually links healing, forgiveness, social inclusion and salvation. All are aspects of the gospel that liberates and transforms not only individuals but the world in which they live.

2 The risen Jesus sends his followers to make disciples of all nations

Matthew 28:5–10, 16–20

This passage has parallels in Mark 16, John 20 and Acts 1, which all contain texts in which the disciples are sent out in mission by the risen Jesus. Matthew's audience are probably Jewish Christians who, like the church in Jerusalem in Acts, still maintain Jewish practice while following Jesus as Messiah. A call to global mission could have been read by Jewish believers as a mission to Jews living throughout the world. Matthew's use of *ethnae* (NRSV: 'nations') is therefore interesting, as in a Jewish context this was the word used to refer to non-Jews. Matthew is writing after the Jerusalem councils mentioned in Acts and Galatians. He therefore knows of the decision that there would be different missions to the Gentiles and to the Jews. Matthew is probably writing to Jewish Christian churches and wants them to realise that the Gentile mission is part of Jesus' commission to the disciples. Sadly, as anti-Jewish sentiment became common in later centuries, the western church would increasingly reject the Jewish churches as heretical. The vision of Jesus to enable faith communities among all peoples became increasingly restrictive and ultimately colonial as Christendom developed in the west.

The language of the second mark of mission – to teach, baptise and nurture new believers – clearly reflects Matthew 28. But what was meant by this teaching? The formula of the second mark of mission could suggest a catechumenate, in which the essentials of faith were taught prior to baptism. But Matthew's Greek suggests something quite different. The word used for 'teach' could have been *katacheo*, suggesting such a catechumenate, but instead we have *didasko*. The choice of the Greek words *entello* for 'command' and *tarein* for 'keep' indicates this is instruction in how to live, not the passing on of doctrine. *The Message* is closer to this than most other translations, with 'instruct them in the practice of all I have commanded you'. Discipleship in this way is more like mentoring new believers than sending them on what is often called a discipleship course.

3 Justice, healing and the salvation of two daughters

Luke 8:40–56

Luke 8 introduces us to two women: one the synagogue ruler's daughter, who we discover has died, and the other excluded from society as unclean due to haemorrhaging. We are given the name of the dead girl's father, Jairus, but as is often the case the two women at the centre of the story are unnamed. Luke's version of this story, also found in Mark and Matthew, is arranged to link the two women. The girl is twelve years old, and the woman had been suffering for twelve years. One is Jairus daughter, and the other is called 'daughter' by Jesus. The connection of daughter and twelve years may be intended to suggest the Jewish custom relating to sons who become 'sons of the Law' at the age of twelve. Indeed, this seems to be behind the story in Luke 2 when Jesus, aged twelve, eludes his parents and is found discussing the law with the teachers in the temple courts.

The text refers to the condition of both women in terms that relate to physical illness and healing. So Jairus' daughter is *apethnesken*, 'withering', and the woman cannot be cured, *therapeuthenai*, by the doctors, but verse 47 tells how she was instantly physically healed, *iathe*, when she touched Jesus' robe. Jesus, however, uses different words: *sesoken* in verse 48 and *sothesetai* in verse 50. These are both forms of the verb *sos*, which can mean 'heal' but is also translated 'save'; hence, 'only believe and she will be saved' (v. 50). The NASB also indicates this possible translation in its footnotes in both cases. This strongly suggests that in verse 48 we are meant to understand Jesus telling the women, 'Daughter, your faith has saved you.'

Both women are restored in a way that is more than a physical healing. Both gain a new life. If this is obvious for Jairus' daughter, raised from death, it is also part of the story of the woman with the haemorrhage. She hides under cover of the crowd because she is unclean due to her condition and thus not allowed to touch others. Her physical healing is not enough; only by publicly exposing her healing can Jesus also restore her to life as a daughter of God among the people of God.

4 Salvation, judgement and changing how we live

Matthew 25:31–46

This parable, unique to Matthew, is controversial, as it apparently suggests we are saved by what we do. Such problems arise when a passage is read out of context and assumed to convey a complete theology. Matthew 24 and 25 contain several parables in which those who will enter the kingdom are divided from those who will not. The point in each is that because the time of judgement cannot be known, one must live in a state of always being ready. Prior to these, Matthew 23 is about the hypocrisy of the scribes and Pharisees, who consider themselves righteous because they tithe but who ignore justice and mercy, which are far more important to God. The scribes and Pharisees are an example of 'goats', who make all the right religious noises but ignore the plight of the poor, the sick and the prisoner. On the outside they look righteous but, as Jesus declares in 23:25, 'inside they are full of greed and self-indulgence'.

In the parable of the sheep and the goats, neither group expects the judgement and neither understands that care for those in need is viewed as an act done to Jesus. This is simply an expression of who they are, not some conscious attempt to win God's favour and a place in the kingdom. In 7:16–20, a passage also about who will enter the kingdom of heaven, Jesus compares people to trees bearing fruit. He says we can tell if they are good if they produce good fruit, which is doing the will of the Father. In a similar way, Paul in his letters talks of the fruit of the Spirit, which is a testimony that the Spirit is transforming us. Genuine repentance leads to changed lives, and judgement exposes whether this has or has not occurred.

I, like many, find the idea of a day of judgement difficult. I certainly think the kind of hellfire preaching that uses judgement to scare people into the kingdom is counterproductive. It can produce people who are professing faith purely for self-preservation. Yet often the poor and oppressed find comfort in these passages because they tell us that there will be justice and that selfishness and the abuse of power will not be allowed to continue. Those who bear the fruit of the Spirit will not be people who only care about outward appearance, but people who care for those in need and seek justice for them.

5 A call to follow and restorative justice

Mark 10:17–31

The three synoptic gospels all contain the story known as 'the rich young ruler'. It seems likely, as is the case in several passages in these three gospels, that Mark is the basis for the accounts in Luke and Matthew. On this occasion, Matthew remains closer to Mark's text while Luke has some variations. All three contain the basic structure of the young man's question, his assertion that he has kept the commandments Jesus mentions, and his turning away sad after Jesus' stipulation that he sell what he has, give the money to the poor and follow him. Mark and Matthew, however, offer a specific detail that Luke has either not understood or has consciously broadened. Where the NRSV has 'many possessions' in verse 22, the Greek in Mark and Matthew has *ktemata*, a very specific kind of possession: an estate of land (hence the NASB: 'he was one who owned much property').

Gerald West, writing on this passage from the perspective of the poor, notes that Jesus does not ask the young man if he has kept the commandment not to covet his neighbour's property. The suggestion is that his large landholding has involved acquiring the land that belonged to others, making them poor. The law of Jubilee was designed to address this by requiring such land be returned. However, the official view was that this law only applied when all the tribes were living in their allotted land, and thus the practice of the Jubilee ended with the exile. Jesus' instruction to the young man to sell the land and give the money to the poor thus acts as restorative justice.

If the evangelistic call to follow Christ involves a change of life, it also involves a devotion to Christ in which wealth of any kind may be a barrier, an alternative master – hence the discussion of the difficulty the rich find in seeking to enter the kingdom. Jesus' emphasis on this clearly troubles the disciples, as does his teaching on divorce earlier in this chapter. They realise that the standard of life Jesus asks for is so demanding that salvation seems impossible. Jesus' response, that this is only possible for God, is of vital importance. Living the life of a follower of Christ is only possible because of God's power, not ours.

6 The new creation and the ministry of reconciliation

2 Corinthians 5:6–21

Verses 16–19 contain a number of issues of translation. Verse 16 says in the Greek, 'We regard no one according to the flesh, even though we once regarded Jesus according to the flesh.' Paul uses *sarx* for 'flesh', which usually denotes the sinful nature, rather than *soma*, which usually denotes the physical body. So, this is referring to us once regarding Christ from a worldly view that was false, hence 'human point of view' (NRSV). Being 'in Christ' changes the way we see Christ and see others. This is because of the 'new creation', which means everything is made new. Translators struggle with verse 17 because part way through Paul simply writes 'if anyone is in Christ new creation'. The Greek contains no such phrase as 'there is' or 'they are', which translations add. For Paul, the new creation breaks in and all is changed. There is a new world and we are called to live in that world where everything is different.

Verse 19 begins with an unusual phrase in Greek, *hos hoti*, 'how that', which is probably used to introduce a quotation: 'in Christ God was reconciling the world to himself'. This quotation can be translated several ways. The most cautious is to see the use of 'in' in verse 19 as the equivalent of 'through' in verse 18 ('God, who reconciled us to himself through Christ'), hence the NRSV's translation: 'that is, in Christ God was reconciling the world to himself'. However, the passage throughout emphasises God reconciling creation and people to himself. Therefore, this sentence is more likely to be concerned with God's relationship with the world and not his relationship with Christ. This makes the translation 'God was in Christ' less likely. There is another possibility, that 'the world was in Christ being reconciled to God'. This may seem strange, but it fits with the idea that Jesus' death and resurrection has instituted a new creation and thus the world is now bound up with him. There is something similar in Ephesians 1:10, in which everything is gathered up in Christ, and Colossians 1:15–17, in which all things hold together in Christ, who is the firstborn of all creation. It is as if the cross becomes the pinch point of an hourglass through which creation flows, the new creation emerging on the other side.

Behind this linking of Jesus and the new creation is Paul's view of Jesus as the new Adam. At the end of Genesis 3 we see relationships broken between humanity and God, men and women, and humanity and creation. Jesus' work of reconciliation mends these broken relationships, and this extends also to creation. In Christ we receive the ministry of reconciliation, and this too extends our mission to creation not just other humans.

Guidelines

- If we have been in church for a while, it is likely that when we have been taught about mission and evangelism. This teaching will have emphasised certain approaches. What has been the emphasis in the teaching we have received? Has the emphasis been on evangelism and seeing people saved or on social action and seeing communities transformed? How much has our church seen the two as connected, and how much has it seen them as separate? What do you feel about this?

- The idea of integral mission is not just that we are called to do both evangelism and social action, but also that you cannot do one and not the other. If we do not have a vision for social transformation, we are not proclaiming the whole gospel; unless individuals are changed by the saving work of God in Christ, society cannot be changed. Do you agree with this? Do you struggle with one or another part of that and if so why?

- The fifth mark of mission, the one with the emphasis on creation, was added later than the rest. This perhaps reflects an increased awareness of environmental issue in society. Do you think this is a key emphasis of mission? What do you think the relationship is between creation care and salvation through Christ? What might such a relationship mean for how I live and how my church acts?

- Social action can be a way of responding to human need with loving kindness, the third mark of mission. A current expression of this would be the running of food banks. But the fourth mark of mission suggests that we also need to challenge the social structures that lead to such need; that is, seeking to change the system so people don't need food banks. This tends to lead to political action. Do you think this is right for churches or should they stay out of political decisions, as some argue?

- How might this approach to mission affect what you say to someone when you are seeking to attract them to become a follower of Christ? What might a message of reconciliation be in today's world? How might it be affected by the context of the hearer, as it was for the rich young ruler? What other contexts might affect that call to be reconciled to God today?

FURTHER READING

Anglican Communion, 'Marks of Mission', anglicancommunion.org/mission/marks-of-mission.aspx.

G. Gutierrez, 'The task and content of liberation theology' in C. Rowlands (ed.), *The Cambridge Companion to Liberation Theology* (Cambridge University Press, 1999), pp. 19–38.

Micah Network, 'Micah network declaration on integral mission', 27 September 2001, micahnetwork.org/sites/default/files/doc/page/mn_integral_mission_declaration_en.pdf.

G. West, 'The Bible and the poor' in C. Rowlands (ed.), *The Cambridge Companion to Liberation Theology* (Cambridge University Press, 1999), pp. 129–152.

World Council of Churches et al., 'Christian witness in a multi-religious world' (28 June 2011), oikoumene.org/en/resources/documents/wcc-programmes/interreligious-dialogue-and-cooperation/christian-identity-in-pluralistic-societies/christian-witness-in-a-multi-religious-world.

Ephesians

Helen Morris

The success of the Harry Potter series, the ongoing appeal of the Marvel movies and the popularity of productions such as *Wicked* and *The Twilight Saga* suggest that interest in the supernatural is high. From a Christian perspective, such interest is not baseless. The Christian faith affirms the existence of both good spiritual beings and those that are malevolent. As C.S. Lewis so perceptively observed in his preface to *The Screwtape Letters*, there are two equal but opposite errors into which Christians can fall in relation to these spiritual powers, particularly the latter type. One error is to refuse to accept the existence of such entities; the other is to not only believe but also to be unhealthily enthralled by them.

The letter to the Ephesians avoids both errors. Writing to Christians in a city obsessed by magic and curses, gods and goddesses, power and experience, Paul acknowledges the spiritual battle that is at play while keeping his eyes, and the eyes of his readers, firmly fixed on Christ. For Christ is not just above every power, authority, rule or dominion; he is in a different league all together. He is the victor who has everything else placed under his feet. And this victor's power is available to his followers. Rather than a life of fear and enslavement to sin and evil spiritual forces, those who trust in Christ are set free. They share in Christ's victory. They are on the winning team. The challenge, then, is to walk in this victory, to live it out in every sphere of life.

Unless otherwise stated, Bible quotations are from the New Revised Standard Version (Anglicised).

1 Chosen in Christ

Ephesians 1:1–14

The notion of chosenness (or predestination) raises the question, What is left of free will if God does the choosing? This question is not easily resolved, but two points of clarification are helpful. First, whenever chosenness is mentioned in the New Testament, it is in the context of reminding the readers of God's sovereignty to reassure them of the security they have in Christ. This is evident in Ephesians 1, wherein Paul interweaves the topic of chosenness with themes such as forgiveness, hope, blessing, love and certainty. Second, this assurance is a spur for action, not an excuse for complacency. Believers should demonstrate their relationship with Christ in confidence, because God is in charge and he is reliable.

With these two clarifications in mind, one way to picture the paradox of God's sovereignty and human responsibility is to imagine that you can only see in 2D. Someone shows you two pictures of a Toblerone: one is a rectangle, the other a triangle. With your 2D vision, you assume that one of these pictures is wrong and the other right. Imagine you can now see in 3D. You realise that both pictures accurately represent a Toblerone, but in a different way than you could have imaged when you could only see in 2D. This analogy helps us understand that references in scripture to God's sovereignty and to human responsibility both represent reality, but, with our finite vision, we cannot understand how they work together. Therefore, we often lean towards one end of the paradox: either God is in charge and we cannot make responsible choices, or we can make responsible choices and God is not in charge. It is helpful to consider, therefore, whether there is one side of this paradox that we find ourselves leaning towards and, if so, why this is and how we might bring greater balance to our understanding.

2 The fullness of Christ

Ephesians 1:15–23

Clinton Arnold describes Ephesians as having a 'power motif' (p. 1). Paul emphasises Christ's supremacy over every rule and authority, power and dominion. This is clear. What is less clear is the description of the church that follows: 'which is his body, the fullness of him who fills all in all' (v. 23).

What does it mean for the church to be the fullness of Christ if Christ fills everything? Isn't everything then his 'fullness'? Exploring how the concepts of fullness and filling are used elsewhere in Ephesians sheds light on this question. The notion of filling brings to mind the temple, indicating that fullness in Ephesians refers to God's glory and presence in its most tangible manifestation. Therefore, fullness is a relational entity; it refers to God's dwelling with his people and revealing his nature to them.

Alongside the meaning of fullness, Paul's focus on both the current blessings that believers receive in Christ (often referred to as the 'now' of God's kingdom) and the future hope that awaits his return (the 'not yet' of God's kingdom) is significant. Christ is 'head over all things' (v. 22), but the believers are to look forward to the time when all things are united under his headship (1:10). The church is Christ's fullness (v. 23), but Paul prays that believers will be filled to the measure 'with all the fullness of God' (3:19). The church is Christ's body (v. 23), but must build itself up in love, growing into 'the full stature of Christ' (4:13–16). With this 'now' and 'not yet' framework in mind, the meaning of verse 23 becomes clearer. When Christ returns, the whole of creation will experience his presence and glory in its fullest manifestation. For now, the church, though imperfect, is the special locus of this power and presence. The church provides a foretaste of what will, in the fullness of time, be true of all creation. As such, it bears witness to Christ's work of reconciliation and the hope found in him.

3 Seated with Christ

Deceit and entrapment often go hand in hand. For instance, who would choose to get into thousands of pounds of debt? Yet the seductive promise of high-odds gambling can deceive people into thinking that the opportunity to win is worth the risk. What starts as a hobby can soon become an ensnaring addiction. A high-stakes win seems the only solution to spiralling debt, only to result in loss, more debt and the cycle continuing.

Deceit and entrapment also characterised the magical practices prevalent in Paul's day. Magical charms, invocations to various gods and goddesses, curses laid upon opponents, amulets and spells were common ways in which those in the Greco-Roman world endeavoured to manipulate supernatural powers to their own ends. Appeasing the 'powers' in this way seemed to bring protection. However, as Paul warns, it actually results in slavery and fear. The 'ruler of the power of the air', whom Paul's readers used to follow (v. 2), is 'the devil' (4:27; 6:11) or 'evil one' (6:16). Slavery to such malevolent powers keeps people trapped in disobedience and so subject to God's wrath. Not that all disobedience can be blamed on demonic beings. Human beings' own self-seeking desires (v. 3) and the influence of the culture and ways of the world (v. 2) also play a part. This is the bad news.

The good news is that Christ's victory brings freedom from all three corrupting entities: the devil, the self and the world. Like all good rescues, this is a rescue with a 'from' and a 'to'. Believers are rescued from judgement, sin and deceptive spiritual powers; they are rescued to a new life in Christ, wherein they are incorporated into his victory.

Paul has this victory in mind when he depicts believers as seated in the heavenly realms with Christ. In this description, Paul is not denying believers' earthly existence, but reminding his readers that they are to live on earth as citizens of heaven. Such a perspective leads to a new way of seeing and living in the world and to 'good works' that God has prepared beforehand for his people to do (v. 10).

4 The peace of Christ

Ephesians 2:11–22

Paul turns his attention from deceitful and entrapping spiritual powers to a more unlikely foe, the law and its commandments, which is what the 'dividing wall' (v. 14) broken down by Christ primarily refers to. However, there is a close connection between the law and the physical barriers of both the curtain separating off the Most Holy Place and the wall between the Jewish and Gentile areas of the temple. An allusion to these divisions surely lies in Paul's mind, shedding light on the problem of the law. It is not the law per se that is at fault, but the way in which it has contributed to people's separation from God and each other. It is not explicit that this is because the law highlights people's rebellion against God, but Romans 7:7–25 is informative here. The destruction of this wall of hostility signifies both the vertical (people with God) and horizontal (people with people) aspects of Christ's reconciliatory work. Both Jew and Gentile can know restored relationship with God and healed relationships with each other.

It is hard for readers today to appreciate the extent of the enmity that there was between these two groups (Jew and Gentile) and, therefore, the power of Christ's peace. If Christ's work can bring reconciliation between these two entities, there is no racial, age, gender or social divide in our day that cannot be similarly overcome. Crucially, though, it is unity not uniformity that Christ achieves. Cultural differences between Jewish and Gentile believers are relativised and transformed in Christ, not obliterated.

The church today must recognise, therefore, that true unity is not monochrome. Rather, in Christ and through the power of his Spirit, the church is to facilitate unity that preserves and celebrates healthy differences. Such unity and diversity should be encouraged *within* individual church congregations. Oscar Cullmann argues that the goal of unity in diversity also applies *across* congregations. Different Christian confessions have particular gifts that are a blessing to the wider body. These gifts should not be abandoned in the name of homogenisation, Cullmann urges, but preserved and nurtured.

5 The mystery of Christ

Ephesians 3:1-13

'Mystery' might, at first glance, seem an odd choice of word for Paul to use to describe God's great plan of redemption worked out in Christ (compare 1:9–10; 4:8). Outside Judaism, a 'mystery' usually referred to some secret knowledge that only those initiated into certain pagan religions and cults had access to. Perhaps, though, this is one of the factors that prompted Paul's use of the term. In contrast to the carefully guarded mysteries known only to the selected few, God's mystery, though once hidden, is now proclaimed loudly and proudly, such that even 'the rulers and authorities in the heavenly places' can see God's wisdom in it (v. 10).

Paul is both a recipient of this revelation and someone who has faithfully passed on the revelation to others. Given the magnitude of God's grace and power, and the unfathomable riches of Christ, why would someone like Paul, who has served God so wholeheartedly, find himself in chains? Paul addresses this question in verses 2–13, which are an explanation of his current circumstances, not, as some have claimed, a defense of his apostleship. Paul suffers to proclaim to the Gentiles 'the mystery' of God's plan for the reconciliation of creation, the fulfilment of which is still a future hope. In his chains, Paul witnesses to this hope through his confident assurance of the transience of his current state and the glory of the future he has inherited in Christ (compare Colossians 1:24–29).

It is easy to fall into one of two errors in relation to the 'now' and the 'not yet' of God's kingdom. On the one hand, we can become overly pessimistic about our current lives and faith, holding Eeyorishly to a dim and distant hope, without any expectation that God might act in the here and now. At the other extreme, we expect the full in-breaking of the kingdom now, with no remainder. This leads to disillusionment when trials and suffering evidence that God has no yet wiped away every tear (Revelation 21:4). Paul holds these two aspects ('now' and 'not yet') in right tension, and he sees their connection. His assurance of God's presence with him in his current suffering bears witness to the reality of his future hope.

6 The love of Christ

I remember as a child hearing a story of a young boy who was given a beautiful vase. As he picked up the vase, he heard something jangle. He assumed this must be money, so he tipped up the vase to get the money out. He shook with all his might, but no money appeared. He tried again to no avail. Eventually, he was so determined to get the money that he smashed the vase against the wall. As the vase shattered, a few pennies dropped to the ground. At that moment he realised the true value of the vase. It was no ordinary vase, but an antique passed down through generations. It would have been worth thousands of pounds were it still intact. The vase itself was the gift, not a few jangling coins that happened to have fallen inside it.

There are two approaches that human beings can take towards God. One is to see worshipping God as an end in itself – indeed, the ultimate end. The other is to see prayer and praise to God as a means to some greater end: a better job, a new relationship, an improved quality of life, a more peaceful mental state and so on. God does provide lots of incredible blessings. He also answers prayer, often in amazing ways. However, when we see our relationship with him as simply a means to obtain certain gifts, we are smashing the vase to get to the pennies. The Bible calls this idolatry: elevating God's gifts higher than God himself.

Paul's prayer in our reading challenges such an approach to God. God's power at work in believers achieves far more than they can ask or imagine. But central to Paul's prayer is an uppermost desire that, beyond anything else, his readers know God – the height, breadth, width and depth of his love – and, in Christ, are filled to the measure with God's presence. Such revelation must surely lead to worship of God and a recognition that even the greatest of God's created gifts is completely surpassed and overwhelmed by the splendour and majesty of the creator himself.

Guidelines

The first three chapters of Ephesians locate the church in the context of God's cosmic plan for the restoration of his creation. From this perspective, the high calling of the church comes into sharp focus. The peace and reconciliation that Christ works in the church is a foretaste of the cosmic shalom (peace and wholeness) that will define the new heavens and new earth. The church consists of believers who were once dead, but are now alive. It is made up of those who used to be far from God, but are now near. As high as Paul's view of the church is, however, he is not naive or unhealthily triumphalistic.

As we'll explore in next week's notes, the second half of Ephesians demonstrates that Paul is not blind to the church's current weaknesses and imperfections. Indeed, he addresses various character flaws that were presumably exhibited in the lives of those to whom he is writing. His emphasis in the letter, though, particularly the first half, is on the great blessings that the church has received in Christ: intimacy with God, the infilling of God's Spirit, future hope and so on.

It is easy in the messy reality of many of our churches' lives to lose sight of this cosmic perspective on the church's identity and calling. How, as Christians, can we hold in right tension the reality of sin and imperfection in the current lives of Christ's followers *and* the glorious picture of the church painted by Paul in these first three chapters of Ephesians? What changes are induced in your own thinking, words and behaviour by reflecting on Paul's description of the church in Ephesians 1—3?

1 The body of Christ

Ephesians 4:1–16

This passage contains several important and intriguing features. I'll highlight two. First, there is the 'therefore', emphasising that any instructions Paul now gives are rooted in his previous exposition of who God is, what God has done and who the believer is in light of God's work (Ephesians 1—3). This feature of Paul's rhetorical strategy, to found his arguments first and foremost in the nature and acts of God, brings to mind A.W. Tozer's well known assertion that, 'What comes into our minds when we think about God is the most important thing about us.' As Tozer goes on to note, 'We tend by a secret law of the soul to move toward our mental image of God. This is true not only of the individual Christian, but of the company of Christians that composes the Church. Always the most revealing thing about the Church is her idea of God' (p. 1).

Second, it is interesting to note Paul's adoption, and adaptation, of Psalm 68:18 in verse 8. Whereas Psalm 68 describes God, the victorious king, receiving tribute from his enemies, Paul cites this psalm in reference to Christ giving, not receiving, gifts. A number of explanations have been proposed for Paul's amendment of 'receive' to 'give' in this citation, often appealing to alternative translations of the psalm. It is more likely, however, that this is yet one more example of the startling reconfiguration that Paul sees obtained through the Christ-event. Not only are two opposing groups, Jew and Gentile, reconciled into one body in Christ (2:15), but those who were formerly God's enemies now receive gifts from him (v. 8). Indeed, as the passage continues, we see how these two outcomes are connected. The nature of the gifts that God's former enemies receive is significant; they are gifts that help build up the one, reconciled body of Christ in love. In other words, those 'who were far off' (the Gentile believers) are not just united with 'those who were near' (the Jewish believers, 2:17); they also play a key role in the one body's growth.

2 Maturity in Christ

Ephesians 4:17–32

The human body is a powerful image with which to promote unity in a social group. Paul was not the only one to use this metaphor. In the fourth century BC Plato used the analogy of an injured finger, which causes pain to the whole body, to argue that societies best flourish when individuals see themselves as part of an interconnected whole (*Republic*, 5.462c–d). So too, writing shortly after Paul, Plutarch argued that those who are divided are like feet that trip each other up (*Moralia*, 478–79). Paul is unique, however, in his contention that the church is not just *a* body; it is *Christ's* body.

Paul beautifully develops this image of the church as Christ's body in 4:15–16. In these verses, he describes the church growing up into its head, Christ, who knits the body together, as each part does its work to build up the body in love. In our reading, Paul fleshes out what this looks like in practice through his imagery of putting off the old self and putting on the new. The old self, Paul notes, is characterised by ignorance, hardness of heart, greed, impurity, promiscuity, delusion, dishonesty, bitterness, ingrained anger, theft, slander, malice and vileness. The new self conforms to Christ's example. It is characterised by right thinking, righteousness, holiness, truthfulness, honest work, generosity, encouragement, kindness, compassion and grace. As believers, through the power of God's Spirit, put off their old selves and put on their new Christlike selves, the body grows in maturity in Christ.

Paul's metaphor of putting off and putting on is powerful rhetorically. It is worth reflecting further, though, on what this might look like in our own lives. We might, for example, put off the old self by confessing areas of sin, such as bitterness or lust, to a trusted friend and asking them to pray that God's Spirit empowers growth in this area. If a believer is watching pornography online, they might put off the old self through both confession and a practical act, such as setting up accountability software on their computer. The exercise of spiritual disciplines can help us put on the new self, such as meditating on scripture and praying daily for the transformative power of God's Spirit to grow Christlike character in us.

3 Gratitude

Ephesians 5:1–20

In yesterday's reading Paul lists opposing pairs to illustrate the difference between a person's old and new self: truthfulness replaces dishonesty; forgiveness pushes out bitterness; right thinking takes the place of ignorance. Therefore, in verse 4, following Paul's denouncement of impurity, crude speech and greed, one might expect an extolment of purity and self-control. Instead, Paul exhorts his readers to thankfulness. Has Paul just moved on from his previous pattern? On the contrary, he is encouraging his readers to see gratitude as the opposite of not just the vices in verse 3, but of all the vices he has so far warned against.

People respond to God in one of two ways. A person can, in faith, trust that God is good and the source of all good gifts. If this is our response, then, regardless of our current situation, our orientation towards God, our default setting, as it were, will be thankfulness. Even in difficult times, we will trust that God is good and that his grace is sufficient. Alternatively, a person can disbelieve in the existence of God and/or* his goodness. If we disbelieve in God's existence or goodness, we search for a 'good' apart from him. In other words, we're back in the garden of Eden, wondering with Eve if God is really a mean-spirited killjoy, withholding power, knowledge and gifts. We choose, with her, to trust our suspicion more than his promises. So we wallow in bitterness and self-pity, overindulge in food or drink, selfishly put ourselves before others and entertain lust or any other such vice to fill the void only God can fill. As Augustine put it, God has made us for himself, and our hearts are restless until they rest in him (*Confessions*, 1.1.1.). The solution? Sustained reflection on the vastness of God's love and goodness, which leads to gratitude.

(*'And/or' might seem odd here. How can you doubt God's goodness if you don't believe that he exists? I'd counter that, in order to disbelieve in God, you have to have a concept of 'god' that you're choosing to reject. It's possible to conceptualise a good, gracious and loving God that you just don't think exists. Often, however, the 'god' a person disbelieves in is, to their mind, of dubious character anyway and this, at least in part, contributes to their disbelief.)

4 The bride of Christ

Ephesians 5:21–33

Household management was a prominent concern in the Greco-Roman world. The order was well established: a man rules over his wife, his children and his slaves. Aristotle, for example, pits a wife's obedience, which is her duty, against a husband's role to command – albeit he argues that a man's rule over his wife is of a different nature to his rule over his children and his slaves (*Politics*, 1259a–60a). Read in this context, the countercultural nature of Paul's exhortations is apparent. Paul's instructions for a wife to submit to her husband are prefaced by his call for mutual submission (v. 21). In addition, his instructions to wives are not, as per Aristotle, matched by an enjoinder for husbands to rule over their wives, but for husbands to love their wives with the same self-sacrificial love with which Christ has loved the church (v. 25). Therefore, Paul's analogy of Christ and the church modifies and challenges the household order as it was understood and implemented in his wider culture.

However, not only does the Christ–church analogy shed light on Paul's vision for marital relationships, so the marital relationship, specifically the intimacy of the married couple as 'one flesh', sheds light on Christ's relationship with the church. The image of the church as Christ's bride is one of a number of metaphors that the New Testament authors use to depict the church (other images include people, body and temple). Paul Minear argues that these images highlight different aspects of the one underlying reality that constitutes the church. That one reality, Minear argues, is God's redemptive work, in Christ and through the Spirit, in drawing people to himself. The metaphor of the church as Christ's bride highlights powerfully the love and intimacy that is at the heart of this relationship.

5 Dignity in Christ

Ephesians 6:1–9

In relation to the Torah (the first five books of the Bible), Iain Provan argues that both idealism and realism are evident in these texts, and good interpreters will take right account of both elements. The ideals of loving God and loving neighbour, he contends, are worked out in and through the various commandments contained within the Old Testament law. However, these ideals are balanced with the reality of a world broken by sin. God meets people where they're at and moves them forward, but he does not legislate the perfection of God's kingdom into being. For example, regarding Old Testament laws on slavery, Provan argues that these laws recognise the existence of slavery and, although they don't abolish this human ill, make radical steps towards improving slaves' rights and experience.

This balance of idealism and realism, Provan contends, provides a model for good law-making today. Laws that are overly utopian, failing to take account of the reality of human sin and the concrete circumstances within which the laws have to be implemented, are not as beneficial to society, or as effective, as those that do take these factors into account (pp. 267, 272).

We see similar idealism and realism in Paul's household code as it continues in Ephesians 6. In these verses, as with Paul's instructions to husbands and wives, there are notable countercultural elements within Paul's exhortations. The tempering of the father's authority, by Paul's appeal that they don't provoke their children, provides a significant qualification to Paul's instructions to children that they honour their parents. The pertinent reminder that God is Lord of both a slave and the slave's master, and has no partiality, is also noteworthy. This relativises and regulates a master's exercise of authority over his slave. Rather than validate slavery, these exhortations sow the seed for later abolition movements. In addition, Paul's encouragement to slaves that, in serving their masters, they can really serve Christ, should not be overlooked. In this, Paul demonstrates that, even in a broken world, in the dehumanising situation of slavery, a person can have the dignity that being a worshipper of God affords.

6 Spiritual armour

Ephesians 6:10–24

Paul invokes military metaphors in this section of his letter. Reference to armour, particularly shields and swords, brings to mind forceful and violent battles. It would seem logical, therefore, that this armour is needed so that believers can withstand the might, or power, of the devil. But this is not what Paul writes. Rather, it is the devil's deceitful scheming that Paul urges his readers to stand against. This disjunction is not to be glossed over. Through it, Paul reminds his readers that the devil's main weapons are not power and strength, but deceit and accusation. We see this in the garden of Eden, where the snake exaggerates God's command: 'Did God really say [is he really so mean and unreasonable] that he would put all this delicious fruit around you and not let you eat from any of it?' When Eve challenges the snake, his exaggeration turns to a blatant lie: 'You won't die [he's not protecting you, he's protecting himself]'. The armour is perfectly suited to rebuff this deceit. The shield enables believers to trust in God's goodness and love. The belt helps them discern falsehood. The helmet and breastplate protect believers from the devil's accusations. The sword and shoes make it clear that this armour is to put believers on the offensive, not the defensive.

Paul's rhetoric of spiritual armour captures the imagination. We must be careful, however, that our description of the believers' fight doesn't stop there. Paul's instruction to pray is also central to his argument in this passage. In a world focused on achievement, productivity and efficiency, the challenge to carve out time to pray can be great. It is easy to get so caught up in the day's to-do list that speaking to God in prayer gets overlooked. Paul challenges such thinking, reminding us of the power and necessity of cultivating a lifestyle and disciplined habit of prayer.

Guidelines

In the first half of Ephesians, Paul reminds his readers of their identity in Christ and the blessings found in him. In the second half, Paul outlines various implications of believers' new identity for their day-to-day lives. In the context of the church, although those with certain gifts have a particular role to play, every member is to help the church grow towards maturity in Christ. In addition, all believers are to live in accordance with the new life they have received and to put off the self-centred and corrupt habits of their past. In family relationships, the love and example of Christ is to direct how members view and treat each other. In order to live rightly in response to the truth revealed in Christ, believers are to take up the spiritual armour and pray, so that they are not led astray by the devil's deceit.

Examining Ephesians as a whole, it is therefore apparent that Paul rightly maintains the paradox between God's sovereignty and human responsibility. When a person is made a new creation, this is the work of God in Christ and through the Spirit. It is an act of sovereign mercy. But this does not mean that a believer is simply passive as they live out their faith. Paul uses lots of active verbs to describe how believers should respond to God's grace: praying, loving, giving thanks and singing, to name a few. How can we, like Paul, also hold divine sovereignty and human responsibility together in the right way? In other words, how do we take responsibility for our own Christian walk while also remembering our complete dependence on God's sovereign mercy and sustaining power?

Paul's prayers in Ephesians guide us in this. It is interesting to note what he prays for. I often find that my prayer times are consumed with problems that I'm asking God to fix, either in my own life or in the lives of those I am praying for. In contrast, Paul prays that his readers will have wisdom, revelation and insight. He prays that they would know God's love and the hope and power found in Christ. Such revelation reminds us of our dependence on God. It also spurs us on to live with gratitude. I'd encourage you to spend time reflecting on these prayers (1:15–23 and 3:14–21) and be guided by them in your prayer life.

FURTHER READING

Clinton E. Arnold, *Power and Magic* (Wipf and Stock, 1989).

Oscar Cullmann, trans. M.E. Boring, *Unity through Diversity* (Fortress, 1988).

C.S. Lewis and Paul McCusker (eds), *The Screwtape Letters & Screwtape Proposes A Toast* (Harper One, 2013).

Paul S. Minear, *Images of the Church in the New Testament* (Westminster John Knox, 2004).

Iain Provan, *Seriously Dangerous Religion: What the Old Testament really says and why it matters* (Baylor University, 2014).

Klyne Snodgrass, *Ephesians (NIV Application Commentary)* (Zondervan, 1996).

A.W. Tozer, *The Knowledge of the Holy* (OM Publishing, 1987).

Ezekiel 25—48

Bill Goodman

In the previous issue of *Guidelines* we explored the first half of the book of Ezekiel. We observed a man uprooted from Jerusalem and taken into exile in Babylon with others from his community (2 Kings 24:10–17). Reflecting by the riverside on his lost calling to be a priest in the Jerusalem temple, he unexpectedly experienced God's call to be a prophet in exile and to speak to his traumatised people there. It would prove to be a costly calling for him, involving misunderstanding, resistance and bereavement.

Ezekiel's extraordinary vision of God's majestic glory, enthroned on an awesome chariot, showed him that this God was not confined to the Jerusalem temple but free to meet his people anywhere, even here in distant Babylon. In a subsequent vision, he found himself carried back home to the Jerusalem temple, to see the corruptions and idolatry abounding there, which resulted in God deserting this unholy place.

The prophet developed a remarkable preaching style, vivid and visual, laced with dramatic gestures and abrasive, sometimes offensive language. We noticed his emphasis on divine judgement and holiness, as well as on the dangers of using distorted memories of a glorious past as a way to avoid challenges in the present and future. He was trying to dispel the illusions of some of his fellow exiles, who believed that God was somehow being unfair to them and must allow them to return home soon. Like his contemporary Jeremiah (prophesying back in Jerusalem), Ezekiel was seeking to help his people understand a recent disaster and prepare for a greater one to come. Questions about how their God could permit devastation by the Babylonians were undermining faith: had Yahweh, the God of Israel, been defeated? Did Yahweh still care? Was Yahweh fair? There was a danger of the exiles lapsing into paganism or despair.

Among Ezekiel's disturbing and challenging messages we heard reminders of Yahweh's forgiveness and continuing covenant commitment to his wayward people, giving glimpses of hope for the future. In this second half of the book, we shall see these messages of hope grow steadily more prominent.

Unless otherwise stated, Bible quotations are from the New Revised Standard Version (Anglicised) or else are the author's own translation.

1 Seeing the bigger picture

Ezekiel 28:1–19

Jerusalem is now under siege by the Babylonian army (24:2). As Ezekiel and his fellow exiles wait anxiously for news, we find an unexpected interlude. Reverting to poetry, the prophet surveys the nations surrounding his native land and declares Yahweh's word to them.

Prophets traditionally took this kind of role. Kings would employ prophets to get God on their side and to curse their enemies (see 1 Kings 22 and Numbers 22—24, which provides a comical example of the pitfalls of this tactic). However, like other Old Testament prophets, Ezekiel has been subverting this tradition to turn his hearers' expectations upside down, declaring Yahweh's condemnation of his own people, rather than of their enemies.

But now, at their darkest hour, Ezekiel takes on the more traditional role, proclaiming Yahweh's word and protection against his people's enemies. Those who have vindictively delighted in and exploited Jerusalem's current perilous state are also answerable to Yahweh, the God of the whole earth. In addition, visions of the elimination of these traditional enemies suggest hope for the future for Israel.

The port city of Tyre was a major commercial hub for Israel's region. In his lengthy critique of Tyre, Ezekiel depicts it as a trading ship of titanic proportions, proudly sailing the Mediterranean – but ending up a sunken wreck (Ezekiel 27). Next, he recycles Eden imagery found in the Genesis creation accounts, presenting Tyre as a self-styled 'paradise-on-sea' (vv. 11–15). God condemns Tyre – not because trade is bad in itself, but because it has become bound up with greed, exploitation and excessive consumption. Later, Ezekiel's own imagery will in turn be recycled by a New Testament prophet, critiquing the exploitative economic empire of his own day (Revelation 18).

The Eden imagery has led some to wonder whether the primeval fall of Satan is being described in this passage, but Ezekiel's warning is to a king in his own day. It is Tyre's leader who is held particularly responsible for his city's corruption. For all his shrewdness in commerce, this king's over-inflated ego and lack of integrity earn him God's condemnation (vv. 2, 5–7).

At the centre of this collection of oracles against foreign nations (Ezekiel 25—32) stands 28.24–26 – words of hope and assurance for Ezekiel's trau-matised people. God's mission continues, and they remain a key part of it. The divine purpose remains unchanged: that they and all other nations 'may acknowledge that I am Yahweh' (25:7, 11, 17; 26:6; 28:23, 26).

2 Don't rely on the unreliable

Ezekiel 29

Desperate times can breed desperate hopes. As they wait anxiously for news of the ongoing siege of Jerusalem by Nebuchadnezzar, some of Ezekiel's audience are hoping for political salvation. Could an alliance with newly resurgent Egypt, as some of the Jerusalem leaders have been proposing, bring Pharaoh's armies to the city's rescue?

In a sequence of oracles, Ezekiel dashes these false hopes. Egypt has always been an unreliable ally and will prove so again. Relying on Egypt is like leaning on one of the flexible papyrus reeds which grow by its great river: they bend and break, cutting the hand that holds them (vv. 6–7). The prophet depicts the Egyptian ruler as a huge crocodile (or perhaps chaos monster) sprawling in the river Nile. It looks fearsome, but it is no match for Yahweh, who will hook it and haul it out, along with Pharaoh's retinue of lesser fish, to be devoured on the river bank by other hungry creatures (vv. 4–5). It is Yahweh who will do this, yet his appointed fisherman will be the Babylonian king, frustrated by the lack of profit from his long siege of Tyre (compare Jeremiah 46).

Pharaoh is condemned for declaring: 'My Nile is my own; I made it for myself' (vv. 3, 9). As king, he did indeed own the land and its great river. But in claiming to have made it, he was declaring himself to be the divine cre-ator, the very source of Egypt's life. Excessive self-importance and a sense of invincibility are among the delusions which power can bring; this kind of arrogant pretension will not be tolerated by the true creator. The high and mighty will, sooner or later, be held accountable.

Few people in Ezekiel's day could have imagined a world where the awe-some empires of Egypt, Tyre and Babylon had disappeared; yet all these would be distant memories by New Testament times. Part of the prophet's role is to expand people's minds, to imagine the unthinkable. He reminds them of the might of Assyria (31:2–14; 32:22–23), which had also seemed so invincible but was long gone in his hearers' own day. Trusting in even the greatest human power ultimately proves a delusion.

3   Owning responsibilities

Ezekiel 33:1–20

Sometimes we may need a reminder about the nature of our calling. As a new season and different emphasis in his ministry is about to begin, we find Ezekiel reminded by Yahweh of the commission given to him in his initial calling to be a prophet (3:16–21).

God describes the role given to Ezekiel as that of a 'watchman' or 'sentinel' (3:17; 33:7). He is to see himself as like one of the lookouts who guard the borders of his land or patrols the walls of a town. Awake, alert and sharp-eyed, the lookout is equipped with a trumpet for sounding the alarm when he sees potential danger approaching. This is an important role: others need to be able to trust and rely on this sentry as they go about their daily lives. Ezekiel reminds his people that he has been obedient to this calling: they cannot accuse him of having failed to sound the alarm.

Relying on the lookout is important. But those who do so also need to face their own responsibilities. When the alarm is sounded, a response is essential. God looks for a life of consistent holiness and obedience. Rather than banking on (or else despairing because of) their past behaviour, Yahweh's people need to turn to him afresh today and every day (vv. 12–16). Personal choices do matter, and now is always the time to make the right ones.

Previously, when Ezekiel was bringing a similar message, his people were resentfully blaming previous generations for their problems (18:1–20). Now they seem to be taking his message to heart and acknowledging their own failings – with a danger of them sinking into despair as a result (v. 10). As they wait anxiously for news about the siege of Jerusalem, their situation in exile may feel increasingly hopeless. So now they need to hear the good news of grace: a life-giving new start is always possible and is still offered to them (v. 11). Undergirding the relentless challenge of so much of Ezekiel's preaching is that conviction about God's astonishing and continuing mercy. So the prophet urges them to put the past behind them and focus on the present moment. Those who truly repent 'shall surely live, they shall not die' (v. 15).

4 The key change

The prophet keeps ahead of changing times, so that he can help his people through them. Repeatedly he has warned the exiles to prepare for devastating news from home. At last, it arrives. They are joined in Babylon by a newcomer (presumably part of a group deported from Jerusalem), who brings the simple, shattering message: 'The city has been struck down' (v. 21). This brief, stark verse is the turning point of the whole book. God now calls his prophet into a different season of ministry. Ezekiel's strange periods of silence are over; now is a time to speak more freely and hopefully, like a singer switching to a more upbeat key.

Among prophetic books, Ezekiel is unusual in giving a number of precise dates. The prophet tells us that his initial calling happened 'in the fifth year of the exile of king Jehoiachin' (1:1–2: 593BC). Now, over five years later, comes this turning point in his ministry (v. 21: 587BC). The rest of the book, although briefer, will cover at least 14 more years (40:1: 573BC).

Does Ezekiel have colleagues and allies who encourage and help him to keep going? There is no real sign of any in the book, but that may not be the whole story. Now that his grim prophecies of the destruction of Jerusalem have come true, it seems that he becomes more popular, even a celebrity (vv. 30–31). The more encouraging tone of what he is now saying is music to some people's ears. He finds himself acclaimed as something of an entertainer in the newly developing synagogues in Babylon (v. 32). Learning to cope with this unfamiliar acceptance, even popularity, may be the new challenge for him!

Applause and flattery can be seductive to a preacher, but what matters is that lives are changed for the better through hearing the message. Ezekiel senses an unhealthy desire to profit from the ongoing crisis, both among peers promoting his ministry in Babylon (v. 31) and among those left to pick up the pieces in Jerusalem and Judah, who cast their eyes greedily over some of the valuable homes and land now left unoccupied (vv. 24–25). So his new messages may be more upbeat, but they retain a challenge to integrity in daily life; he has not completely changed his tune.

5 Poachers and gamekeepers

Ezekiel 34:1–16

Occasionally we hear stories of former poachers who are transformed into gamekeepers, protecting the creatures they used to hunt. The opposite can also happen. In this chapter, Ezekiel depicts people in power as shepherds, who ought to be protecting and feeding Yahweh's people, the flock entrusted to them. Instead, they are fleecing, neglecting and even slaughtering those for whose welfare they are responsible.

Having drawn on the familiar picture of a sentry on watch in the previous chapter, Ezekiel now chooses another image which his hearers will easily recognise. Shepherds grazing flocks were a common sight; some of his hearers would have experienced this role.

An ambivalent attitude towards shepherds seems to have developed among Jews in biblical times. In their writings, some of the rabbis scorn shepherds as unreliable and dishonest. Yet the shepherd also became a metaphor for God's chosen leaders of the community, particularly kings and religious leaders (2 Samuel 7:7; Jeremiah 23:1–6). Privilege and power are thus turned into a responsibility for providing tender yet also fiercely protective care for the flock (compare Psalm 72:1–4, 12–14). But, frail human beings may become careless, lazy, indifferent, cowardly, greedy and oppressive. Leaders must be held accountable. Corrupt leadership is a scandal seen particularly in the history of Israel's monarchy which earns Yahweh's condemnation (vv. 2, 10).

So what is the alternative? Having no shepherd at all is not the solution: the sheep simply end up wandering aimlessly, scattered and vulnerable (vv. 5–6). Good leadership is still vital. All this highlights the need for a consistent and reliable shepherd, leading on to the image of Yahweh as shepherd (vv. 11–16; compare Psalm 23; 80:1; 100:3). Only Yahweh can be totally relied on to bring salvation, blessing, governance, strength and protection.

This ambivalence about shepherds is reflected much later in Jesus' teaching about the unreliable hired hand who deserts the flock and needs to be replaced by the truly committed shepherd (John 10:11–15). This passage, with its clear echoes of Ezekiel, makes the astonishing claim that Jesus inhabits and fulfils the role of Yahweh as the rescuing, gathering, nurturing, good shepherd (compare Hebrews 13:20–21; 1 Peter 2:25). But the New Testament is also clear that God has not given up completely on human shepherds: Jesus entrusts his sheep to the care of under-shepherds, such as Peter (John 21:15–19; 1 Peter 5:1–4).

6 Covenant commitment

Yesterday's passage highlighted the danger of leaders neglecting or abusing the flock. But leaders cannot be blamed for everything: others can also succumb to the temptations of power. Today's passage suggests there are power struggles within the flock, perhaps arising from the lack of leadership. In this mixed flock, the bigger, stronger rams and he-goats have become greedy and careless, taking the best of the grazing opportunities, satisfying their own appetites to the detriment of others (vv. 17–22). This might refer to earlier generations living in Judah or to contemporaries who have some degree of power among the exiles and are abusing it in a domineering way. There is an ugliness about indifference towards the weak and particularly about bullying; 'survival of the fittest' (or fattest) can never be the way of life in the community of God's people.

The words of Yahweh which the prophet expresses are intensely personal. In ways not always obvious in our English translations, this chapter repeats particular words using emphatic Hebrew forms: 'you', 'he', 'them' and particularly 'I/my' (e.g. 34:7, 9, 11, 20, 24, 30–31). This adds an emotional edge to the outrage, concern and commitment expressed by God to his people. Yahweh's declarations are also framed in an emphatic form, as if to underline that God really does mean business (see 34:15, 31; also 34:7, 24). As ever, Yahweh's goal is relationship: 'Then they will know that I, Yahweh their God, am with them and that they, the house of Israel, are my people' (v. 30). This is not simply about being forced to acknowledge who is boss: the language is personal and relational.

In contrast to the unreliable shepherds, God faithfully seeks his flock (34:6, 8, 10–11). In spite of their waywardness, Yahweh's covenant commitment to them continues (v. 25). Part of that commitment will include giving them new leadership, although this will mean a new 'ruler/prince' – the word 'king' is not used, in light of the failings of so many previous kings (shepherds). In language that echoes Leviticus 26:4–13, they are promised their own land again – and when they are in tune with their covenant Lord, the land will be protected and fruitful. There is real hope for the future.

Guidelines

Judgement

- In the film *Pulp Fiction*, one of the gangsters repeatedly quotes a garbled version of Ezekiel 25:17 as he prepares to execute people. How can we best respond to people who choose to manipulate scripture in order to support their own agenda? It can be dangerous to see ourselves as 'the good guys' who are on God's side, doing God's will. If we identify with God's people Israel, we must remember that they are above all 'a rebellious house' (2:7).

Power

- Ezekiel presents the downfall of the great powers of his day (chapters 25—32). Think of the great empires and regimes of more recent times which are now no more. What light does this shed on today's political situation? What sense of perspective and hope can it bring?

- Ezekiel reminds us that power can corrupt, bringing unhealthy delusions of grandeur to emperors and also more ordinary people, including power struggles and bullying within the community of God's people (compare chapter 34). How then shall we exercise whatever degree of power has been entrusted to us – in our families, churches, communities and the wider world?

Pastoral leadership

- Ezekiel 34 presents images of God's people suffering from neglect or abuse by unreliable leaders and needing a true shepherd. Pray for leaders. If you have a pastoral or leadership role yourself in your church, remind yourself how Jesus fulfils Ezekiel's vision of the true shepherd (John 10). Ask God how you may better reflect the good shepherd in the under-shepherd role which Christ has entrusted to you.

Turning points

- Have you experienced a turning point in church life or in your own ministry: a key moment when a new season began in the life of the church and some new approaches were needed in response? How might you be ready for that kind of experience in future? If it led to a sudden change in your popularity, for better or for worse, how would you handle that (compare chapter 33)?

Responsibilities

- Contemporary western culture has developed a strong emphasis on people's rights – which can be very good news, particularly for persecuted minorities. But Ezekiel regularly reminds people (including himself) to face up to their responsibilities – to God and to each other (e.g. chapter 33). How does that speak to our world today?

1 The mountains of home

Ezekiel 36:1–15

God's creativity and grace finds expression in physical, 'earthy' forms: 'In the beginning God created… and it was good' (Genesis 1); 'He set the earth on its foundations… You make springs gush forth in the valleys' (Psalm 104:5, 10). Divine blessing comes to us clothed in the earthy realities of food, drink, relationships and a gloriously diverse creation. For Israel, the focus of this blessing was in the land given to them.

Here, as earlier in the book, we hear the prophet speaking to 'the mountains of Israel' (see 6:1–14). At that earlier stage of his ministry, Ezekiel warned them of God's judgement; in this new phase, echoing the earlier chapter, his words to the mountains are crafted to bring them hope.

Ezekiel is addressing his hearers among the exiles, using the 'mountains' as a rhetorical device. Yet he depicts God's care for them as bound up with their land. He evokes the mountains, hilltops and ravines, along with the towns and fruitful fields, now abandoned but still fresh in the memory of some who have recently arrived in Babylon. Their sense of dignity and identity and their understanding of God's promises are all inextricably linked with their homeland. They may fear for their own homes and villages – and not without reason, as their traditional enemies in Edom (36:5; also called Mount Seir, 35:1) have applauded Israel's demise and now seek to muscle in on its territory. Chapter 36 proclaims God's refusal to allow this to happen.

The promise is that fruit will be tasted again in future, not by these opportunist interlopers but by 'my people Israel, for they shall soon come home' (v. 8). The humiliated and despondent exiles need to hear Yahweh's promise: 'I am for you' (v. 9). They need to ignore the taunts of their enemies, who depict this promised land as one so prone to bloodshed and famine that it consumes its own inhabitants (v. 13). Such nightmares will happen 'no longer' (a phrase found six times in verses 12–15). A new era is promised; can they dare to believe it?

2 A changed heart and spirit

Ezekiel 36:16–38

We all see the world from our own perspective. We can be tempted to regard ourselves as the centre of the universe – with God being there to meet our needs, perhaps even needing us and our attention. If we fall into any such delusions, Ezekiel can help dispel them. Some of his fellow Old Testament prophets proclaim that Yahweh is motivated by loving care and compassion for his people (see Isaiah 41:8–14; 43:1–4; Jeremiah 31). Ezekiel chooses very different language. For him, Yahweh's primary motivation in restoring Israel is concern for 'my holy name' (vv. 20–23; also 20:9, 14, 39). To drive home the point, that special name, 'Yahweh', is itself found eight times in this passage.

What is this divine self-interest? It stems from the message given by his people, who have 'profaned' Yahweh's name. This refers not so much to blasphemous words, but more to the way their current pitiful state, as landless prisoners of war, brings dishonour to Yahweh. Other nations have misinterpreted Israel's defeat as a sign of Yahweh's weakness. They mock, saying that Israel's god, Yahweh, is not much of a god – either too weak or too indifferent to protect his own people. Marduk of Babylon must be stronger! In such a situation, how can Israel's mission – to make the living God known to all nations – ever be accomplished? Yahweh now decides to waive the rigour of his judgement on Israel, in order to clear his name and vindicate his reputation.

Compared to some of the other Old Testament prophets, Ezekiel may sound harsh. Is he unaware of Yahweh's compassionate love, as proclaimed by Isaiah and Hosea? Can this same Yahweh really also declare, 'It is not for your sake, O house of Israel, that I am about to act, but for the sake of my holy name' (v. 22)? The use of extreme contrasts is a feature of biblical literature, often used to emphasise an important truth (as in Luke 14:26, where Jesus does not actually want people to 'hate' their parents). Ezekiel points away from human need, however keenly felt, directing attention instead to Yahweh's glory and honour. Daniel (9:15–19) takes a similar approach.

But even when Yahweh does return Israel home, a deeper transformation is needed – an internal one. So his grace extends still further, with the promise of shame washed away and the gift of a new 'heart' and 'spirit'. People's thinking and feeling, attitudes and motivations all need renewing by the life-giving breath of God. Repeatedly, emphatically, Yahweh declares that 'I will' do this.

3 New life for the dead

Ezekiel 37:1–14

Ezekiel's preaching tends to be vivid and visual, a style exemplified above all in this passage, his most famous vision. Five times in the first ten verses of this chapter he declares, '*hinneh*' – 'look!' – inviting us to see the vision with him.

As earlier (8:1–4), Ezekiel finds himself carried 'in the Spirit of Yahweh' (v. 1) to a disturbing, creepy place where he sees something truly shocking. The scene suggests a mass slaughter, now long past – the flesh of the corpses has rotted or been stripped by scavengers, leaving only a mass of bones. The dead lie dishonoured – not receiving proper burial was an insult and humiliation in ancient cultures. (As often in Ezekiel, we find echoes of Jeremiah – see Jeremiah 8:1–2.) The feelings of Ezekiel's people are laid bare: catastrophe has overwhelmed them. Sapped of vitality by the trauma of the exile, their hope has died (v. 11).

Then God's tantalising question challenges the prophet: 'Can these bones live?' (v. 3). Ezekiel's guarded response ('You know the answer as well as I do') leaves Yahweh to answer his own seemingly ridiculous question. Or is there a hint of belief in Ezekiel's words, that a miracle might be possible?

The wonderful good news is that Yahweh wants his people back on their feet, and he has the power to bring it about. Intriguingly, Ezekiel himself is the agent of renewal, part of the process God chooses to use, through the words he is commanded to speak to them. Speaking to the dead might feel absurd – yet, crucially, the prophet obeys. And the miracle begins, right before his eyes. But the tension rises: a further stage is needed.

The promise made in 36:27–28 is now visualised before us. The divine *ruach* – 'wind', 'spirit' or 'breath', mentioned ten times in these verses – is essential in order to fully animate God's people. There are echoes here of the Genesis creation accounts (Genesis 1:2 and especially 2:7; see also John 20:22). Here is a new creation, a rebirth of Yahweh's people. God promises to restore their life and hope, to restore them to their land (v. 14), even to reunite the divided kingdoms under one king (see the passage that follows, 37:15–28). Is this an impossible dream – or a vision that can re-energise and inspire?

4 The battle to end all battles

Ezekiel 38

Anxiety and depression can be like invasive species in the garden of the mind, hard to remove once they have taken root. Some of Ezekiel's hearers may be wondering about the future he is promising: 'Even if this miracle does happen, even if God does rescue us and return us to our land – what then? Will we be safe? Surely we'll be a smaller, weaker nation than before, vulnerable to attack and invasion?'

As usual, the prophet seeks to refurbish their scarred imaginations by painting vivid word pictures. He evokes the scariest scenario imaginable: a predatory monster of an enemy, forging alliances with other nations and invading after they have resettled in their homeland. The name Gog is a puzzle to us. It has a mythical feel, perhaps evoking Gyges, a king of recent history notorious for brutal oppression, just as we might speak of another Hitler or Stalin arising.

The invading forces present an apparently overwhelming threat. Yet in all of this, Yahweh is in control. The enemy make their own arrogant decisions; yet God is the ultimate power, somehow directing and using them (vv. 14–16). Gog's 'great horde' (v. 15) will suddenly experience a 'great' earthquake (v. 19) – a display of Yahweh's 'greatness' (v. 23).

The urge to look for signs of prophecy unfolding in the events of one's own day has led to differing interpretations of these two chapters. Luther saw Gog's forces as the threat of Turkish invasion in his day; later, Gomer was seen as Germany, while some contemporary writers have equated Meshek with Moscow and *rosh* (Hebrew for 'head', 38:2, 39:1) with Russia. Bending biblical words out of shape to suit our current political understanding is an urge to be resisted. Those who see literal events here have to explain away the swords, shields, horses and arrows of these verses, which are not the actual weapons of our day. This exotic, larger-than-life figure called Gog may be better understood as something that recurs in history, an archetype (compare Revelation 20:7–10). Evil, in all its recurring forms, may sometimes look formidable and scary, yet ultimately it is destined to fail, after one final great battle. Earth's warmongers come and go, but one day they will finally be eliminated.

5 The glory returns

Ezekiel 40:1–5; 43:1–12

Sustaining a long and demanding ministry is a challenge. Almost 20 years have passed since Ezekiel experienced his initial vision by the Chebar river (1:1; 40:1). Now, on this new year's day, he looks to the future – and finds himself once more in his homeland, set down in a city on 'a very high mountain' (40:2). This can hardly be a literal description of Jerusalem, which is lower than some of the surrounding hills; once again, we find the symbolic words and world of a visionary experience.

Although Ezekiel's familiar delight in detail is evident in these long final chapters of the book, they do not provide nearly enough information to be a literal blueprint for builders. Nor is Ezekiel told to 'make', as Moses repeatedly was when given details of the tabernacle (Exodus 25—31). When the Jerusalem temple was later rebuilt by the returning exiles, they did not try to follow Ezekiel's plan. What the prophet offers here is a symbolic, virtual-reality tour of an ideal restored temple, through which he is guided by a supernatural project manager. The incessant measuring of dimensions conveys a sense of beautiful, geometric symmetry with everything perfectly ordered – nothing out of place or crooked. Here is a vision of true worship restored: for Ezekiel, deprived years earlier of his expected priestly ministry, this is the ultimate picture of that long-cherished dream coming true.

The last time the hand of God transported Ezekiel to Jerusalem in a vision (8:1—11:25), he witnessed in anguish the departure of Yahweh's glorious presence – Israel's God was forced out of his own home in the temple by the blatant sinfulness of the people there. Now, at last, the prophet witnesses the reverse: the thunderous, dazzling divine glory returns through that same east gate and fills his house once again (43:4–5). Yahweh is still the free, mobile God of the chariot throne, able to meet people anywhere at any time, but now Yahweh graciously chooses to return home and never desert that special place (43:7 – see also 48:35).

The challenge with this new start is to avoid repeating past mistakes. Yahweh declares that the people must end their unfaithful 'affairs' with other gods, which may have included excessive reverence for the graves of former kings, located in or near the temple complex (43:7–9).

6 A life-giving river

Ezekiel 47

The living God is the source and giver of life. The return of God's presence to the Jerusalem temple brings the restoration of life so abundant and overflowing that it cannot be contained there: it flows out across the rest of the land – even to parts which seem most dry and dead.

Previously, Ezekiel saw a vision of his people as dry bones, miraculously restored to life by the breath of Yahweh (37:1–14). Now comes another surreal, visionary experience of that dynamic power of Yahweh, this time as a river which cleanses their polluted homeland, renewing creation (echoing Genesis 1—2). Flowing from the temple, from the presence of God comes abundant power to refresh and bless. In the course of a short distance (about two miles) this bubbling brook miraculously swells into a deep river, which nourishes 'very many trees… and very many fish' (vv. 7, 9–10), even down in the Dead Sea rift valley region east of Jerusalem. Most gardeners would be satisfied with trees which produced a harvest once a year; imagine trees which have medicinal value in their leaves and provide fruit every month (v. 12)! A later prophet, seeing further visions refracted through the lens of Ezekiel's, would sense the extension of this promise still further, bringing healing beyond the promised land to 'the nations' (Revelation 22:2).

The rest of the book details how the promised land is to be divided when Yahweh's people return to it. Ignoring the geographical features and the instructions given when they first entered the land (see Joshua 13—19), Ezekiel pictures the land neatly carved into strips of equal size. This is not literal but visionary, theological geography: a picture to show God's purpose and expectations for his returning people. From now on, no one may dominate and no one is to be exploited; there must be fair shares for all the twelve tribes (v. 14) – and even for resident foreigners (vv. 21–23). The promise and challenge is of justice and hope for all. At the heart of the nation will be the temple, expressing worship of Yahweh. The centrality of God in all things is underlined in the book's closing words: the city will become known far and wide by a new strapline: 'Yahweh is there' (48:35).

Guidelines

God's good nature

- Think about Ezekiel's distinctive understanding of God as it has unfolded through his prophecies – awesome, free, sovereign; holy and demanding holiness; concerned about Yahweh's own holy name being honoured. How does this fit with your own understanding of God, and your church's understanding? Does Ezekiel's God seem too harsh? Remember also the sense of Yahweh's covenant commitment and desire for personal relationship, which we saw earlier (34:17–21). How balanced is your picture of God's character?

- Where does self-interest fit in? Our own self-interest can lead us to think of God as being there to do our bidding – rather than us being here to do God's bidding. Reflect on Ezekiel's sense of Yahweh's self-interest (e.g. 36:17–38) – God's desire to be known and obeyed. What effect would that bring to us and to our disordered world?

Home: where the heart (and the hurt) is

- Ezekiel repeatedly directs the exiles' attention towards their homeland. They feel a need to belong somewhere, as part of their identity. The longing for home is a powerful instinct in our own day, not least for many who are landless, stateless or refugees: they need support, particularly from those of us who have homes. How best can we offer our support?

- Focusing on home can raise another question: where is God at home? In Ezekiel's visions we see Yahweh being forced out of his rightful place by the idolatry of those who claimed to belong to him (chapters 8—11) – but then eventually returning home, restored to the central place at the heart of the community (chapter 43). What do these pictures say to you as an individual and to your church community?

New life for the dead

- Do you ever feel like you are 'preaching to the dead', as Ezekiel was called to do (37:9)? Yet the prophet sees those dry bones come alive, revitalised by the breath/spirit of God. He also sees that life-giving river flowing from the throne of God, bringing fruitfulness to the driest, dead places (47:7–12). New life is given, even to the dead. Pray for this to happen through your life and ministry, as the living waters of the Holy Spirit overflow from your life and bring God's blessing to others (compare John 7:37–39).

FURTHER READING

Leslie Allen, *Ezekiel 1—19* and *Ezekiel 20—48* (Word, 1990).

Walter Brueggemann, *Out of Babylon* (Abingdon, 2010).

Corrine L. Carvalho, *The Book of Ezekiel: Question by question* (Paulist, 2010/2016).

John Goldingay, *Lamentations and Ezekiel for Everyone* (SPCK, 2016).

Paul M. Joyce, *Ezekiel: A commentary* (T&T Clark, 2007/09).

Christopher J.H. Wright, *The Message of Ezekiel* (IVP, 2001).

Proverbs (Part II)

Ernest Lucas

In our previous issue of *Guidelines*, we saw that 'wisdom' in Proverbs is 'the ability to cope with life in the best possible way'. In seeking to inculcate this ability, the Hebrew sages were not just concerned with imparting knowledge and skills but with the formation of character. Like all good teachers, they used a variety of approaches and techniques in their teaching.

As a way of grounding their teaching in real life, they created a variety of characters who illustrate different virtues and, more often, vices. These are sometimes sketched in a cartoon-like manner, occasionally with an element of humour. In the first week of studies, we will look at a selection of these characters.

The dominant literary form in Proverbs is the two-part sentence proverb. This, itself, can take different forms. Sometimes the second half of the sentence expresses a contrast with the first, for example, 'Hatred stirs up strife, but love covers all offences' (10:12). Most of the proverbs in chapters 10—15 have this form. Sometimes the second half repeats the essential point of the first in different words, for example, 'Pride goes before destruction, and a haughty spirit before a fall' (16:18). In another variant, the second half extends what has already been said, for example, 'A fool takes no pleasure in understanding, but only in expressing personal opinion' (18:2). Sometimes the sentence contains a striking comparison, such as, 'Like cold water to a thirsty soul, so is good news from a far country' (25:25). In the previous set of notes, we saw that in Proverbs 1—9 the sages also used another literary form, the 'instruction'. In the second week, we shall look at examples of other, less common, literary forms that occur in Proverbs.

Unless otherwise stated, Bible quotations are from the New Revised Standard Version (Anglicised).

1 The wise

Proverbs 3:5–8; 9:9–10

The fundamental characteristic of 'the wise' is that they are godly people, because for the Hebrew sages wisdom is based on 'the fear of the Lord' and 'knowledge of God' (1:7; 2:5; 9:10; 15:33). This means having a personal relationship with God which is marked by trust in, and obedience to, God (3:5–8). It is compared to the relationship between a loving father and the son in whom he delights (3:11–12).

Teachability is the most frequently mentioned attribute of the wise in Proverbs. Wisdom is not just something innate. It needs to be acquired through 'instruction' and 'training' (1:2–3), and this is not easy. It is an ongoing process (9:9). This requires a readiness to accept 'discipline' and 'reproof/rebuke' (3:11–12; 6:23; 10:17; 12:1), as well as advice (12:15; 19:20). Willingness to undergo this process calls for humility (15:33).

The second most mentioned characteristic of the wise is the way they use words. Through their speech they spread wisdom and knowledge to those ready to accept it (13:20; 15:2, 7). Their teaching becomes a 'fountain of life' to others (13:14) and their words bring healing to those who need it (12:18). The wise choose their words carefully so that they are judicious and persuasive (16:23). Instead of inflaming a situation, they know how to calm it down (15:1; 29:8). One aspect of being judicious is to know when to stay silent, so the wise person exercises restraint in speech (10:14, 19; 12:16, 23).

Another attribute of the wise is best expressed in English, as usually in the NRSV, by the word 'prudence' (it also uses 'shrewdness', 'good sense', 'deals wisely' and 'clever'). This is now rarely used in everyday language, though it was once acceptable as a personal name because it expressed a desirable quality. The Hebrew words used express the ideas, according to context, of discernment, discretion, forethought and practical understanding. Woman Wisdom lives with prudence and urges people to learn it (8:5, 12). It is shown by the wise son who works hard to gather the summer harvest (10:5), an example of contingency planning to provide for any possible future crisis (22:3). The prudent wife who knows how to run a household well is a gift from the Lord (19:14). Prudent behaviour can lead to success for both the royal official (14:35) and the household servant (17:2).

2 The fools

One purpose of Proverbs is to teach prudence to 'the simple' (1:4, NRSV has 'shrewdness'). In Proverbs, the simple person is someone who is gullible, willing to believe anything (14:15) and so is easily led astray. It is a dangerous state, which easily leads to folly: 'The simple inherit folly' (14:18, NIV, following the Hebrew text, which the NRSV emends). The contrast in this verse shows that the basic weakness of the simple is lack of knowledge. Woman Wisdom describes them as 'without sense' (9:4), a phrase that might be translated as 'empty-headed'. Their state is not a hopeless one if they will respond to her offer and learn from her.

Two main words are translated as 'fool' in Proverbs: *kesîl*, 49 times and *'ewîl*, 19 times. The closeness in their meaning is shown by the fact that the same word is used for the 'folly' that characterises them both. Both, of course, lack wisdom (putting *kesîl* references first, 14:33; 1:7) and reject the instruction and correction that are essential to growth in wisdom (17:10; 15:5). They lack self-control, as shown by being hot-tempered (29:11; 12:16).

The distinctive of the *kesîl* is their resistance to the discipline of learning. They want to acquire wisdom the quick and easy way by buying it, but are not seriously committed to learning (17:16). The fact is that they think they know it all already (28:26) and so are not interested in learning from others, but only in expressing their own opinions (18:2). This resistance to learning means that what little wisdom they have is either ineffectual (26:7) or harmful in its effects (18:6; 26:9).

The root of the *'ewîl*'s folly is expressed in more explicitly moral and spiritual terms. They despise parental instruction (15:5), and the implication of Proverbs 1:7 is that this attitude is related to not having 'the fear of the Lord'. Proverbs 14:9 probably means that they make light of sin.

It is easy to refuse to see ourselves in unattractive portraits like these, but the sages remind us that we can exhibit the vices of the fools: 'Do you see persons wise in their own eyes? There is more hope for fools than for them' (26:12); 'Do you see someone who is hasty in speech? There is more hope for a fool than for anyone like that' (29:20).

3 The lazy person

Proverbs 6:6–11; 24:30–34; 26:13–16

The 'lazy person' (or 'sluggard', the more picturesque term used in the NIV and others) is one of the minor characters in Proverbs. In their references to such people, the sages show their sense of humour. They depict them as a figure of tragi-comedy, a butt for their satirical wit.

Proverbs 26:13–16 paints a comic picture of them as unwilling to respond to the demands of life. On waking up, they re reluctant to leave their bed. They are 'hinged' to it like a well-oiled door. With a vivid imagination, they invent preposterous excuses (further exaggerated in 22:13) for not getting up and going out. When brought food, perhaps breakfast in bed, they are too lazy to feed themselves (19:24). Yet, in their delusion, they are full of self-satisfied smugness.

The consequences of this approach to life, never making the effort to get to grips with the demands of today and postponing everything to tomorrow, or beyond, because it is too much trouble, are depicted in Proverbs 24:30–34. The picture of a neglected, and therefore unproductive, vineyard is no doubt a metaphor for a wasted life. The practical result is poverty, because there can be no harvest if there has been no ploughing and planting of crops at the right time (20:4), a metaphor that can apply to a variety of activities necessary for supporting life. The sages warn that such laziness can have disastrous consequences (21:25). For this reason, the sages try to get some sense into the lazy person by urging him to observe and learn from the behaviour of the ant (6:6–11). It is self-motivated and diligent, not needing anyone to make it get on with its work.

These vignettes bring out various characteristics of lazy people. They are unwilling to take the decisive step to start anything, always making up excuses, however unconvincing, for inaction. They will not finish things because that takes too much effort. As a result, they suffer from unsatisfied desires (13:4; 21:25) and are helplessly trapped in the mess they have made of their lives (15:19). The lazy person is unemployable, because giving such a person a job to do will only lead to irritation and frustration (10:26) or worse (18:9).

Procrastination, the sages warn, is a stupid (24:30), potentially fatal (21:25), approach to life.

4 The whisperer and the gossip

Proverbs 2:12–15; 6:16–19

Liars and lying are strongly condemned in the book of Proverbs. 'A lying tongue' is listed as one of seven things that 'the Lord hates' and that are 'an abomination to him' (6:16–19) and 'lying lips' are also said to be 'an abomination to the Lord' (12:22). Lying to someone is characterised as a form of hatred for the victim (10:18; 26:28).

A particular example of the liar in Proverbs is the character called 'the whisperer'. This person is bracketed with a 'perverse person' (16:28) who is described in some detail in Proverbs 2:12–15, depicted as someone who delights in turning truth on its head. The whisperer, then, is someone who surreptitiously spreads falsehoods. This poisons relationships and creates strife, even separating close friends (16:28). The sages blame the whisperer for stoking up quarrels like someone adding wood to a fire (26:20). It is a sad comment on human nature that too often we enjoy listening to the words of the whisperer. The sages compare this to enjoying swallowing a tasty morsel (18:8; 26:22). People enjoy a piece of juicy talebearing and are all too ready to believe it. The trouble is that, once accepted and believed, the whisperer's words are not easily forgotten. Like food, they become part of us, imprinted in our memory, and affect our view of the world and other people. That is why the sages warn that listening to such a perverse talebearer is as bad as being one (17:4).

Another character, 'the gossip', can be seen as an overt whisperer, spreading false tales more openly. In Proverbs, this person is particularly linked with revealing secrets (11:13). People are warned that it is best to avoid the company of the gossip (20:19).

In biblical times, these characters spread their falsehoods by word of mouth. Now, thanks to social media, their falsehoods can be spread farther and faster than ever before. A piece of 'fake news' or a malicious rumour quickly reaches millions of people. The major social media platforms are urged to find ways to prevent or control this, but there seems no easy way to do so.

5 The scoffer

The 'scoffer' or 'scorner' is one of the most frequently mentioned minor characters in Proverbs. Their essential characteristic is arrogant pride (21:24). For this reason, the scoffer is contrasted with those who are humble (3:34). Although mentioned in parallel with the fools and the simple (1:22), the essence of the scoffer's problem is not, like them, lack of mental capacity; it is their mental attitude. They are full of conceit and utterly self-opinionated, as shown by their refusal to accept any kind of correction. Those who try to correct them are met with abuse, even hatred (9:7–8). The only value to be gained from attempting to discipline or punish the scoffer is the lesson that the simple might learn from observing how scoffers deserve to be treated (19:25; 21:11).

Humility and willingness to accept correction are essential to growth in wisdom, so it is not surprising that the scoffer seeks wisdom in vain (14:6). This proverb can be understood in two ways. It may mean that when scoffers finds themselves in a difficult situation and needs wisdom to cope with it successfully, they will not have the inner resources to be able to do so. Their personal opinions, of which they are so proud, will not meet their needs. Alternatively, it could mean that, should a scoffer decide that it would be useful to acquire some wisdom, perhaps because it might bring some power or prestige, hey will not be able to acquire it because they lack the teachability to do so. For example, they are not willing to go and learn from the wise because they are not prepared to accept their rebukes (15:12).

The scoffer's arrogance does not only harm themselves; it provokes quarrels and abuse and causes trouble in the community (22:10; 29:8). It is not surprising that scoffers bring down condemnation on themselves and may be repudiated by their community (19:29; 24:8–9). However, the worst thing of all is that they are scorned by God (3:34).

The attitude that our ideas and opinions are better than those of anyone else is a pitfall into which we can all fall from time to time, sometimes with serious results. The sages provide the best antidote to it: 'Do not be wise in your own eyes; fear the Lord and shun evil' (3:7).

6 The righteous and the wicked

The most frequently mentioned group in Proverbs is 'the wicked'. Many proverbs contrast them with 'the righteous/upright'. They desire evil (21:10) and regard those who act uprightly with loathing (29:27). They act shamefully (13:5) but brazen it out (21:29). Some of their characteristic traits are: arrogance (21:4), lack of mercy (12:10; 29:7), covetousness (21:26), disdain for the moral law (28:4), perversion of justice by using bribes (17:23) and perverse use of speech (10:32). They violently reject any attempt to rebuke them (9:7).

The righteous, by contrast, desire what is good (11:23) and loathe those who act unjustly (29:27) because they give thought to how to exercise justice (12:5). They care about the rights of the poor (29:7) and about the proper treatment of animals (12:10). They hate lying (13:5) and are careful in the use of words, thinking before they speak (15:28) and seeking to say what is wise and appropriate to the situation (10:31–32). As a result, what they say builds people up (10:21). Hence their words are as valuable as 'choice silver' (10:20).

Understandably, the greatest contrast between the wicked and the righteous is seen in their relationship to God. The wicked are among those who do not fear the Lord (10:27). They and their household live under his curse (3:33). Their way of life is an abomination to the Lord and so, therefore, are their sacrifices (15:8–9). Because they are separated from him, God does not heed their prayers as he does those of the righteous (15:29). In fact, he thwarts their desires (10:3).

The relationship between the righteous and God is sometimes expressed in intimate terms. When Proverbs 3:32 says that the righteous are in God's 'confidence', the Hebrew word used means that they are in his circle of trusted intimates, close friends. God loves the righteous (15:9). He blesses their homes (3:33) and provides for their needs (10:3). He protects the righteous, being their 'strong tower' where they can find security in times of difficulty and danger (18:10).

Proverbs 4:18–19 depicts the lives of the righteous and the wicked as being as different as light is from darkness. Paul describes Christians as not being in darkness but being 'children of light and children of the day' (1 Thessalonians 5:5), and he urges his readers to 'live as children of light' (Ephesians 5:8).

Guidelines

In Proverbs there are about the same number of sayings that refer to 'the righteous' as there are that refer to 'the wise'. Since being wise involves 'the fear of the Lord' and 'knowledge of the Holy One' (9:10) it might be assumed that the terms 'the righteous' and 'the wise' are synonymous, interchangeable. However, a detailed study of their use in Proverbs shows that, rather than being synonymous, they are co-referential. This means that the terms themselves do not have the same sense but may apply to the same referent. In Proverbs, being 'wise' and being 'righteous' are different, though somewhat overlapping, concepts. Both can, and ideally should, be characteristics of one individual. In reality, one individual may display these two sets of characteristics to different degrees. The challenge of Proverbs, with its integrated spirituality, is that godliness has different facets, and all of them need to be well developed to produce the jewel of an attractive godly person. It is not good enough to think that because I am strong in one or two aspects of godliness, I need not work hard at developing others. Prayerfully meditating on the virtues and vices of the characters portrayed in Proverbs is a helpful way of carrying out a check-up of one's growth in godliness.

Study of the characters in Proverbs, and we've looked at only a selection, raises important pastoral questions. How far does your church encourage and help people develop the virtues of the good characters? How would it cope if one or more of the bad characters began to attend regularly? The character portraits in Proverbs are, of course, somewhat exaggerated and cartoonish. In reality, some of the vices of the bad characters probably do exist to some degree even among your church members. Are they recognised and how are they dealt with? It would be an interesting and helpful exercise for groups of people involved in pastoral care in the church to meet and study the bad characters in Proverbs and then move on to discuss what pastoral issues they raise and how these can be dealt with. This would involve both how to help someone to overcome a bad trait and how to help other people cope in a positive way with the person concerned.

1 A proverb cluster on planning wisely

Proverbs 16:1–9

Most people regard Proverbs 10:1—22:16 as a random collection of sentence proverbs lacking any structure. A few scholars have recently argued for the existence in this section of deliberate clusters of proverbs, marked out by various literary and grammatical features and some thematic coherence. Proverbs 16:1–9 is an example. Divine sovereignty and human planning are the theme of both verses 1 and 9, forming an 'inclusio' ('brackets'), a literary device that marks out a section of the text. This is reinforced by another literary device called a 'chiasm': the order of the key Hebrew words in verse 1 ('plans – mind – man [humans]') are reversed in verse 9 ('man [humans] – mind – plans'). What, then, is the coherent message of this cluster if the proverbs in it are taken together?

Although verse 1 is sometimes taken to mean 'Man proposes, God disposes', it is more nuanced than that. The antithesis of the two body parts, 'heart' (rightly taken to mean 'mind' in NRSV) and 'tongue', is a Hebrew way of expressing the totality of human activity. The proverb does not denigrate human planning but stresses that human dependence on God is necessary for success in carrying out plans. What follows develops this. God knows our true motivations better than we do (v. 2) so we must be humble with regard to our plans and actions. The whole process must be submitted to God (v. 3). The Hebrew syntax of the first half of verse 4 is ambiguous. The proverb is probably saying that God's sovereign control will ensure that wicked behaviour is punished. Verses 5–8 expand on verse 2 by describing behaviours of which the Lord does and does not approve. Arrogance prevents a person depending on God and so is 'an abomination to the Lord'. By contrast, loyalty, faithfulness and reverence towards God keep people from doing evil, and make forgiveness possible if they do sin (vv. 5–6). A right relationship with God leads to harmonious human relationships, which improves the likelihood of success in carrying out plans (v. 7). Verse 8 gives another example of a behaviour that pleases the Lord. The cluster is rounded off by verse 9, which returns to the theme of verse 1 but expands its application from individual projects to a person's whole way of life ('the way/the steps').

2 Some Egyptian-style proverbs

Proverbs 22:17–21, with its call to be attentive to wise teaching (vv. 17–18) and statement of purpose (vv. 19–21) introduces a new section in Proverbs, which continues to 24:22. Hebrew proverbs normally consist of a two-part sentence. In this section, the proverbs are four-part sentences, a characteristic of Egyptian proverbs. This section, especially in 22:17—23:11, has similarities to an Egyptian book called *The Instruction of Amenemope*, dating from around 1200BC. Many scholars think that this section of Proverbs is modelled on that book, though also drawing in proverbs from elsewhere.

Amenemope has 30 short chapters, not just 30 sayings (v. 20). In calling for attentiveness, it urges the readers to let the proverbs 'rest in the casket of your belly.' In Hebrew, verse 18 calls on the readers to 'keep them [the proverbs] in your belly' and adds a specifically Hebrew theological motivation for the teaching. Amenemope's purpose is to enable the student 'to know how to return an answer to him who said it, and to direct a report to the one who has sent him', which is similar to verse 21.

Amenemope's first admonition starts, 'Beware of robbing a wretch, of attacking a cripple.' The admonition in verses 22–23 not to rob the poor or treat the afflicted unjustly (legal disputes were heard 'in the gate') is similar but has a Hebrew theological motivation. In Proverbs, the angry 'hothead' is one of the bad characters people are told to avoid (vv. 24–25). Amenemope warns against associating with the angry 'hot-mouthed man'. The rather humorous admonition against acting as a loan-guarantor (vv. 26–27) picks up a theme that runs through Proverbs but not Amenemope. The maintenance of ancient boundary markers (v. 28) is also urged in Amenemope. In verse 29, a rhetorical question stresses the importance of being skilful in work in general. Amenemope is more specific: 'The scribe who is skilled in his office, he is found worthy to be a courtier.'

The Hebrews believed that the principles of wisdom were embedded in the order of creation and are available to all who seek wisdom diligently with humility (8:22–36). Therefore it is not surprising that they accepted that sages in other cultures who sought to understand how to cope successfully with life in an open and honest way would discover genuine wisdom which the Hebrews could appropriate.

3 A poem on sustainable living

The two-part sentence that is the normal form of the Hebrew proverb is also the basic unit of Hebrew poetry. This passage is one of the few poems in the book of Proverbs. It has been understood in different ways. The key issue is the interpretation of verse 24, which is the basis for the admonition in verse 23, and on which verses 25–27 expand.

The message of the first part of verse 24 is clear: stored-up wealth will not last forever; money is a diminishing resource. Since elsewhere the sages warn that hastily amassed wealth can disappear as quickly as it is gained (13:22; 28:22), some see here a warning that money made quickly by trade and commerce is not to be relied on. However, the warning against relying on stored-up wealth could apply as readily to the farmer who has had a bumper harvest or has built up big herds, like the 'rich fool' in Jesus' parable (Luke 12:13–21). The emphasis seems to be on the more general principle of relying on sustainable resources rather than on hoarding wealth. Trade and commerce, as well as agriculture, can be pursued in sustainable ways. The mention of a 'crown' in verse 24 suggests to some that the agricultural imagery of the poem should be taken metaphorically. Rulers in the ancient Near East were often regarded as the 'shepherd' of their people, so the poem might be about ruling well and making wise use of national resources, both human and material. However, the 'crown' here need not be a royal one and could refer to a desire for social status, perhaps based on amassed wealth. This, too, is an unreliable asset.

The poem is best taken at face value. It encourages the wise use of renewable resources to provide a sustainable lifestyle. Making hay at the right time from the grass grown over winter allows new grass to grow following the spring rains. Additional fodder can be gathered from uncultivated land. Well-fed and well-tended animals provide the household with the food and clothes that it needs. Any surplus can be sold to buy new land to expand the farm. This sustainable approach to living can be applied to other forms of livelihood and its implementation is urgently needed in the face of our current ecological crisis on planet Earth.

4 The words of Agur

Proverbs 30:1–9

All that we know of Agur and his father comes from this passage. Their names are non-Israelite. The strong allusions in verse 5 to 2 Samuel 22:31 and verse 6 to Deuteronomy 4:2, to speeches that contain the mature counsel of David and Moses, respectively, suggest that this passage presents the wisdom of an elderly sage.

Comparison of modern English translations shows that the meaning of the start of Agur's utterance is uncertain. The NRSV gives one of the most likely renderings. The Hebrew word used for 'stupid' or 'brute' (v. 2) is a strong one, indicating a level of understanding no better than that of an animal (as in Psalm 73:22). Agur declares his lack of wisdom and knowledge of 'the Holy One' (v. 3, NRSV footnote, recognising the plural as a 'plural of majesty'), God. This is the humble confession of someone who has faced up to the complexities of life with honesty and expresses his perplexity in somewhat hyperbolic language. He has no simple, cut-and-dried answers.

The questions in verse 4 can be compared with those used in Isaiah 40:12–14 and Job 38—39 to expose the limits of human understanding and the inaccessibility of divine wisdom. The first and fourth refer to the vertical and horizontal limits of the cosmos and the two in between refer to major natural forces. The implied answer to the rhetorical questions is, 'No human, only God.' The second part of the fifth question is odd since people are normally defined by their parents, but that would not be appropriate for God. Maybe the 'child' is humanity.

Verses 1–4 are often seen as expressing scepticism. It is more plausible that they are a vivid expression of the limitations of human knowledge, which is found elsewhere in Proverbs (21:30; 25:2; 27:1). Since only God has, and can give, reliable knowledge, God's word is to be accepted and trusted. To add to it is to claim to have true wisdom independently of God.

Agur's prayer (vv. 7–9) is the only one in Proverbs. The idea of balance and moderation that it expresses is a recurrent theme in Proverbs (17:27; 25:16–17, 27–28). Agur uses the personal name of the God of Israel (v. 9, 'Yahweh'). He has moved from a position of doubt and uncertainty to a sense of personal relationship with him.

5 Some 'number proverbs'

This is a series of five 'number proverbs' interspersed with two that are not. The origin of this form of saying may be an interest in observing and classifying natural phenomena and human behaviour, which was an integral part of ancient Near-Eastern wisdom. The pattern 'x things… x+1…' may express completeness or put emphasis on the final example. The sayings focus on aspects of life from which lessons can be learned, but those lessons are not pressed home, leaving the reader to ponder them and tease them out.

The four insatiable things form contrasting pairs: Sheol (death)/womb (life); water/fire. The insatiability of the womb probably refers to the deep desire of a barren woman for a child, especially in a society where this was important for economic and social reasons. The comment about the land reflects the hot, arid summer of Palestine.

In verses 18–19, what the sages find 'too amazing' is the 'way/manner' in which the four things move. The exact cause of wonder is unclear, partly because of debate over whether the final line refers simply to sexual attraction or sexual intercourse. Is the wonder due to the movement in each case having no visible cause? However the saying is understood, it makes the point that much in the world lies beyond full human comprehension. The sayings before and after it are linked to it by catchwords. The Hebrew word for 'vulture' in verse 17 is translated as 'eagle' in verse 19 and the word 'way' links verse 20 to verse 19.

The sages saw the cosmos as a unity. Chaos or harmony in one aspect of it affected the whole. Verses 21–23 are about the behaviour of four kinds of people (two male, two female) who gain power unexpectedly. Significantly, they recognise that life does not always follow the pattern that the sages' teaching elsewhere presents as the norm.

The four wise creatures (vv. 24–28) demonstrate 'life skills' (lizards are welcome because they keep down insects) which are the essence of wisdom. Wisdom is more important than size or strength.

In verses 29–31, the identity of the second creature is uncertain, as is the translation of the final line. The ESV rendering, 'a king whose army is with him', is to be preferred to that in the NRSV. The point seems to be the importance of exhibiting confidence and strength.

6 An acrostic poem: 'the worthy woman'

Proverbs 31:10–31

This poem is an alphabetic acrostic; the initial consonant of each verse follows the order of the letters in the Hebrew alphabet. This may be intended as a memory aid or to convey the sense of completeness in covering the topic. It is about a woman who is a rarity (vv. 10, 29). The meaning of the adjective used to describe her in verse 10 is hard to convey. It is often used in the sense of 'strong, courageous' as applied to warriors. It can denote someone who is considered 'of worth' because of their abilities or moral qualities or wealth. This poem presents a woman who is 'worthy' because of her practical abilities and her moral (v. 20) and spiritual qualities (v. 30).

Some feminists view this poem with ambivalence, suggesting it praises a woman who lives to advance male interests and well-being. Many others, however, emphasise the positive portrait of the woman: her business acumen, administrative abilities, strength, independence and wisdom. Some regard it as subversive of male dominance and empowering for women because, although the setting is domestic, it enables people to conceive of women acting beyond that sphere. Perhaps it is not intended as a picture of any actual woman but as a composite image of the attributes and activities that women in general may have and do.

Verse 30 is not a condemnation of charm and beauty (5:19 commends them in a wife). Using the hyperbole that often features in Hebrew proverbs, it points out that they may be deceptive and ephemeral and that the most important attribute a person can have is 'the fear of the Lord'. Significantly, this verse echoes the 'motto' of the book (1:7) as it rounds it off. In Proverbs 1—9, wisdom is personified as a woman. At the end of the book, wisdom is 'incarnated' in a woman, showing that the wisdom taught in the book is practical and liveable and leads to well-being in life. Proverbs is addressed to men, 'sons'. It is not difficult to imagine this poem transposed into one addressed to women about a 'worthy man' who incarnates the attributes of wisdom. Psalm 112, an acrostic poem about a man who fears the Lord, provides a template. It does not major on 'macho' qualities but on moral and spiritual virtues similar to those attributed to the 'worthy woman' of Proverbs.

Guidelines

In the 'Words of the Wise', 'Words of Agur' and elsewhere in Proverbs, the Hebrew sages were willing to appropriate wisdom from outside Israel, even from worshippers of gods they regarded as false, as in the case of the Egyptians. Their theological basis for doing this is one we share. Do we show the same humility and openness to learn from those outside the church? The Protestant reformer John Calvin believed that, since God is the only source of truth, it is only because of God's 'common grace' that humans can ever discover truth of any kind. Honest seekers after truth are led to discover it in various areas of knowledge because the Holy Spirit leads them to it. Therefore, Calvin argues in his *Institutes of the Christian Religion* (Book 2, 2.15), Christians who ignore or reject truth from non-Christian sources risk offending the Spirit of God.

It is humbling that long ago the Hebrew sages showed a concern to promote sustainable living that has been largely lacking in western societies, especially since the Industrial Revolution. Sadly, many Christians have been opposed to, or suspicious of, the 'green movement'. Happily, there have also been Christians who have responded positively to it, for sound Christian theological reasons, and Christian organisations that have become active in promoting green issues, including sustainable living. Is your church registered as an 'eco church'? If not, go to the Eco Church website and see the resources they have to enable Christians 'to care for creation, to love our global neighbours, and to follow God faithfully'. It is also worth pondering what the practical implications might be of taking seriously Agur's prayer for God to enable him to live a moderate lifestyle.

Because Proverbs is male-centred, being the advice of a father to his son preparing him for life in the wider world, it does raise gender-sensitive issues. However, as noted in our reading of the poem about the worthy woman, it is often not difficult to do some gender transposition of the teaching to express a female-centred perspective. The suggestion of writing a poem about the worthy man, perhaps using Psalm 112 as a guide, would be a profitable exercise for an individual or a group.

FURTHER READING

R.J. Clifford, *Proverbs (Old Testament Library)* (John Knox Press, 1999).

Ernest Lucas, *Exploring the Old Testament, Volume 3: The Psalms and wisdom literature* (SPCK, 2003), chapters 3–4.

Ernest Lucas, *Proverbs (Two Horizons Old Testament Commentary)* (Eerdmans, 2015).

R.C. Van Leeuwen, *Proverbs (New Interpreter's Bible, Volume 5)* (Abingdon, 1997).

Strangers, others, neighbours

Helen Paynter

Drawing on psychoanalytic theory, Julia Kristeva describes how people groups form societies of exclusion. The presence of strangers among us provokes a feeling of anxiety, related to our inability to categorise them. We struggle to place their behaviour, dress, customs and worldview within our own frames of reference. The world becomes unpredictable to us. Our response to this anxiety is *abjection*.

In abjection, we *split* from ourselves those within our midst who make us uncomfortable, those who threaten our preferred self-image. We establish boundaries between those we have abjected and ourselves, and across these boundaries we *project* the negative aspects of ourselves which we wish to reject. This process of splitting, projection and abjection becomes for us a means of creating our own ideal identity. We affirm ourselves based on what we have rejected; as Kristeva puts it, 'lives based on exclusion' (J. Kristeva, *Strangers to Ourselves*, Harvester, 1991, p. 6).

The boundaries that we establish may be real or representational; they may be national borders, the barbed-wire fences of detention facilities, ghettoes or simply psychological barriers. We tend to seek out and gather with those who are like us, and we ascribe to those who are not like us negative motives, habits or other characteristics. We define ourselves by what (or who) we are not. This is the process of *othering*.

The life of Jesus is characterised by his refusal to engage in othering. He was persistently found hanging out with the people in the group that society had abjected. In our reflections for the next fortnight, we will be investigating what is meant by the principle, set out in both Old and New Testaments, that we should love our neighbour. This is an exploration of hospitality.

Unless otherwise stated, Bible quotations are from the English Standard Version (Anglicised).

1 Do we, don't we?

3 John 2–10; 2 John 7–11

The importance of hospitality to the early church is easy to demonstrate. Paul commends it to the church in Rome, alongside peaceable living and inclusivity to the poor (Romans 12:9–21). Peter urges it in 1 Peter 4:9. It is one of the core virtues listed as a prerequisite of overseers (1 Timothy 3:2; Titus 1:8). Hospitality is expected of widows hoping to be supported by the church (1 Timothy 5:10). And Jesus anticipates that those who travel with the gospel can reasonably expect to receive hospitality (Matthew 10:9–15, 40–42).

But it is easy to assert the biblical imperative to hospitality without being honest about the counter-examples, and the counter-instructions. The tension is well illustrated by these two excerpts from the Johannine letters, most likely penned by the same author and certainly originating from the same community. The exhortation to hospitality in 3 John is counterbalanced by the dire warnings against welcoming those who teach heresy in 2 John.

What are we to make of such an apparent contradiction? The key is in the words used to describe those being offered or refused hospitality. In 3 John, although 'strangers' (v. 5), they are 'brothers' (vv. 3, 5, 10). In 2 John, it is 'deceivers', who deny the incarnation (v. 7) and go beyond the teaching of Christ (v. 9), who are to be rejected. But in the ancient world, the offering of hospitality to a travelling teacher was more than a nicety to make his stay more pleasant; it was to enable the ministry itself. Compare Paul's words to the church in Rome: 'I hope to see you in passing as I go to Spain, and to be helped on my journey there by you, once I have enjoyed your company for a while' (Romans 15:24). Indeed, we see this idea in the Johannine letters also. Those who welcome the brothers will be their 'fellow workers' (3 John 8). But the one who is hospitable to the heretical teacher 'takes part in his wicked works' (2 John 11).

We should also notice that both of these instructions about hospitality are framed within the context of how to and whether to welcome fellow believers (or at least, those who claim to be). They may be strangers, but they are still brothers. To discover an ethic of welcoming the true stranger, the *other*, we will have to look elsewhere.

2 Creation hospitality

Genesis 2:5–25

Do not be deceived by the language of 'work' (vv. 5, 15). Unlike the other ancient Near-Eastern creation myths, in the Genesis story humankind is not created to be the slave of the deity. The words 'work' and 'keep' (v. 15) are the same pair of verbs used of the role of the priests in the sanctuary (Numbers 3:7–8; 8:26; 18:5–6; depending on your version they may be translated 'serve'/'minister' and 'guard'). And in Genesis 1, the divine blessing and mandate expresses human purpose in terms of vice-regency (vv. 27–28).

Far from being slaves, Genesis 1—2 makes it clear that humans are placed in the garden as an act of hospitality by God. As chapter 2 tells it, the garden was created for the man, complete with 'every tree that is pleasant to the sight and good for food' (v. 9). It is watered by four rivers (vv. 10–14), and the land that they irrigate is enriched by gold and precious stones.

Everything is made by God for humankind's benefit; this is divine hospitality. God is choosing to limit himself in order to make room for the created world; it is a supreme act of hospitality or, as Reinhard Hütter puts it, 'the sharing of the divine life with those who are dust' (Hütter, 'Hospitality and truth: the disclosure of practices in worship and doctrine' in *Practicing Theology: Beliefs and Practices in Christian Life*, ed. Miroslav Volf and Dorothy Bass, Eerdmans, 2002, p. 219).

Similar language is used of the land of Canaan when the people of Israel take possession of it. This is 'a good and broad land, a land flowing with milk and honey' (Exodus 3:8), with bunches of grapes that took two men to bear (Numbers 13:23–24), and 'great and good cities that you did not build, and houses full of all good things that you did not fill, and cisterns that you did not dig, and vineyards and olive trees that you did not plant' (Deuteronomy 6:10–11).

We may have questions about the occupation of the land of Canaan by the nation of Israel; we might very well have issues about the means by which it takes place. But these are matters for another time. Here, we see the rich theme of divine generosity; the earth was given to humanity and the land was given to the covenant people. We are recipients of divine hospitality. 'What do you have that you did not receive?' (1 Corinthians 4:7).

3 Hospitality as a response to slavery

Deuteronomy 24:14–22

The appeal to the memory of slavery is often made in the Torah. In the Deuteronomy passage we read today, there are two examples of this. Justice must not be denied to the alien or the orphan, because of the recollection of Egyptian slavery (vv. 17–18), and provision is to be made for the destitute alien, for the same reason (vv. 19–22).

Why is the story of ancient slavery to be ethically formative for Israel? First, because redemption from slavery was an act of God, and this brought Israel into covenant with him under his sovereignty. Second, because there was a cultural memory of the experience of oppression, and this recollection ought to ingrain compassion into the warp and weft of the nation.

But, in an unexpected twist, this theme of hospitality is to be extended even to Israel's erstwhile oppressors. 'You shall not abhor an Egyptian, because you were a sojourner in his land. Children born to them in the third generation may enter the assembly of the Lord' (Deuteronomy 23:7–8).

For Jewish philosopher Emmanuel Levinas, this outrageous welcome is a paradigm for the generosity of God's people. He uses this verse and two others to demonstrate the astonishing command of hospitality towards Egypt, the erstwhile enemy. 'Kings bear gifts to you… Let bronze be brought from Egypt' (Psalm 68:29–31, NRSV); 'Praise the Lord, all nations! Extol him, all peoples!' (Psalm 117:1).

How can the nation which oppressed and enslaved Israel be permitted to bring gifts to the Messiah of Psalm 68? How can Psalm 117 countenance that the Lord receive praise from all peoples – even Egypt? Because, says Levinas, the psalmist remembers that:

[Egypt] is the country of servitude, but also the place where Abraham and Jacob found refuge in time of famine; where Joseph was able to assume universal political and economic responsibilities at the very core of Holy History; and where, at the hour of exterminating cruelty, Pharaoh's daughter saved Moses from the waters.

Emmanuel Levinas, *In the Time of the Nations* (Athlone Press, 1994), pp. 97–98

And, ambiguous as to whether he is referring to Israel or Egypt, Levinas adds: 'To shelter the other in one's own land or home, to tolerate the presence of the landless and homeless on the "ancestral soil,"… is that the criterion of humanness? Unquestionably so' (p. 98).

Such unexpected grace and generosity should be the defining characteristic of the people of God.

4 Levitical myth-busting: entitlement

Leviticus 25:1–34

In the immigration debate which continues to rage in this country, two 'facts' are frequently offered as unassailable. They are used so frequently, and with such conviction, that they have become part of the national myth, by which I mean a notion that enters the national consciousness to shape its perception of how the world is and why that is so. Leviticus 25 encourages us to challenge both myths, and we will consider one today and one tomorrow.

The first myth which we hear all the time at the moment is usually phrased along these lines: this is our country, and these are our resources. Acceptance of this as fact usually leads to a discussion about whether the resources in question should or could be shared with outsiders.

Initially, Leviticus 25 may appear to support the notion, 'When you come into the land that I give you…' (v. 2). However, our English translations do not well convey the Hebrew's emphatic use of the first-person pronoun: 'When you come into the land that *I* give you.' The land is a gift from God. But later in the chapter, the emphasis is upon God's ownership of both land and people: 'The land shall not be sold in perpetuity, for the land is mine. For you are strangers and sojourners with me' (v. 23); 'For it is to me that the people of Israel are servants. They are my servants' (25:55). In a passage which is really all about the rights – or otherwise – of the landed over the landless, of the free over the bonded, this emphasis is surprising.

Of course, we can't drag-and-drop this on to our own situation. Leviticus was written for ancient Israel, not us. And Israel was established with a divine promise of physical land (Genesis 15:18–21). Later in the story, the events of exile, the words of the prophets and the coming of Jesus will develop that into a spiritual reality. But at this point in the story, land is central to who Israel is and what God is doing in the world. And yet here, the Torah emphasises to the people of God that they do not own it at all. If even Israel could not regard herself as having entitlement to the land and its resources, how much less may we, to whom no such promise has been made?

5 Levitical myth-busting: the neighbour

Leviticus 25:35–55

A second myth of our time is related to the first. It is usually expressed something like this: we should look after our own people (the citizens of our own country) before we think about needy foreigners. Our own poor are our first priority. But once again, Leviticus 25 challenges this: 'If your brother becomes poor and cannot maintain himself with you, you shall support him as though he were a stranger and a sojourner, and he shall live with you' (v. 35).

The 'sojourner' (*ger*) was a resident alien, not to be confused with the 'foreigner' (*nokri*). The foreigner was a non-Israelite who was not a part of the community and to whom hospitality might be offered. But the sojourner had made his or her home within the people of Israel. They were potentially very much part of the out-group: vulnerable to exploitation and poverty. These laws about how to treat sojourners were not about hospitality so much as social justice.

According to verse 35, then, if a fellow Israelite became destitute, he was to be treated kindly, in the same way that sojourners were treated. The passage then goes on to set out the provision which the sojourner may reasonably expect: notably, not to be exploited. This is in accordance with a number of other places in the Torah where it is stated that the resident alien should be treated on parity with the native Israelite (Exodus 22:21; 23:9; Deuteronomy 1:16; 24:17).

Admittedly, there are other places where the treatment of resident aliens is less equitable (even within this chapter: vv. 44–46). Nonetheless their treatment was expected to be more generous than might be expected in an ancient society. And here, at the heart of this jubilee manifesto, when the writer is looking for a means of expressing the generous treatment due to an impoverished native Israelite, he chooses to liken it to the treatment of a sojourner, an 'other'. This is an extraordinary reversal of expectations. Treat the in-group as well as you treat the out-group.

6 Purity of blood?

Ezra 10

The Old Testament nation of Israel is often characterised as being one of fixed boundaries, of rigid ethnic borders. Certainly there are moments in biblical history that would give support to such a view; this chapter of Ezra would be one of them.

One of the questions to ask when we wrestle with one of these challenging texts in the Old Testament is: where is the divine voice to be heard? There is nothing in this story that tells us God's opinion of Ezra's actions. We are to draw our own conclusions.

As a counter-narrative to that of ethnic purity, there are remarkable episodes of inclusion of foreigners into the nation of Israel. Indeed, full membership of the nation seems to have been far more flexible than it first appears. At the defining event for the nation of Israel, the exodus from Egyptian slavery and miraculous escape through the Red Sea, the departing Hebrews were accompanied by many of non-Israelite origin (Exodus 12:38). In Joshua, we find the extraordinarily juxtaposed narratives of Rahab, the pagan who escapes the ban to find a welcome in the midst of the nation (literal translation of Joshua 6:25), and Achan, the Israelite who comes under the ban through his disobedience (Joshua 6—7). The Torah makes provision for non-Israelites to join fully in the religious life of the nation, observing the sabbath (Exodus 20:10), and even – once circumcised – participating in the Passover (Exodus 12:48–49; Numbers 15:15–16).

There are many more examples of such blurred boundaries: we could consider David's request for Moabite hospitality and protection for his family (1 Samuel 22:3), or the highly unexpected and often hospitable attitude displayed towards Aram (Syria) during the time of Elisha (1 Kings 21:15—2 Kings 8:15). Even the strongly anti-Nineveh polemic of Nahum is counterpoised with the extraordinary story of God's tenderness towards Nineveh in the book of Jonah.

As with the case of ownership of the land, here too the modern imperative is striking. If even Israel, whose identity is closely bound up with the 'seed' of Abraham, is porous at its boundaries, there can be no biblical justification in our modern world for any ideology based upon blood purity.

Guidelines

- If offering hospitality in the ancient world was an enabling of the ministry of the guest, what might be the equivalent of such actions in our day? And, bearing in mind 2 John's warning against collusion with false teaching, what might we need to avoid?

- Hospitality and welcome are framed in the Old Testament as being the appropriate response to the prior generosity of God. How should our own receipt of divine grace and generosity shape our response to the 'other'?

- Most churches in the UK are still fairly monocultural. How should such a local church respond to the increasing diversification of the community it serves? A typical response is to aim to be welcoming and accepting; a laudable aim in itself, of course. But if 'inclusion' simply means acceptance on one's own terms and an expectation of absorption into one's own church culture, is this yet another example of neocolonial colour blindness?

1 Poor, blind, lame

Leviticus 21:16–20; Luke 14:12–24

The Dead Sea Scroll 1QM describes the eschatological battle as viewed by the Qumran community. As part of the description of how this will be conducted, it says, 'No lame, blind, paralysed person nor any man who has an indelible blemish on his flesh, nor any man suffering from uncleanness in his flesh, none of these will go out to war with them.'

The Qumran community is, of course, reflecting the restrictions upon who was permitted to serve in the tabernacle, as set out in Leviticus 21. From this duty the blemished, the blind, the lame, the hunchbacked, the leprous and the eunuch were excluded.

This slightly inconsistent list of the excluded is reflected, again with slight variations, in Luke's gospel, where it is not a marker of out-group membership, but serves as a roll call of those who were the particular subject of the divine invitation. So, for example, when the imprisoned John the Baptist loses his nerve and sends to Jesus to enquire if he really is the Messiah, the message that is returned explicitly references these excluded people: 'Go and tell John what you have seen and heard: the blind receive their sight, the lame walk, lepers are cleansed, and the deaf hear, the dead are raised up, the poor have good news preached to them' (Luke 7:22). The inherently excluded are being drawn into the circle of those who receive blessing.

The great banquet described by Luke can be compared to the eschatological banquets envisaged by the writer of the Aramaic Targum on Isaiah 25. The original description of the eschatological banquet in Isaiah is characterised by its broad and generous welcome: 'On this mountain the Lord of hosts will make for all peoples a feast of rich food, a feast of well-aged wine, of rich food full of marrow, of aged wine well refined' (Isaiah 25:6). However, the divine generosity is tightened up in the Targum on the same passage: 'Yahweh of Hosts will make for all the people in this mountain a meal; and though they suppose it is an honour, it will be a shame for them, and great plagues, plagues from which they will be unable to escape, plagues whereby they will come to their end' (Aramaic Targum on Isaiah 25:6).

Into this theological milieu strides Jesus, welcoming the poor, the crippled, the lame and the blind, and extending the invitation of the eschatological banquet to them all.

2 Reverse contagion

Leviticus 15:19–30; Mark 5:24–34

Many readers will remember, as I do, the frisson of horror and delight that ran around the press for a couple of days when the Princess of Wales visited a London hospital in 1987 and touched patients dying of AIDS with her ungloved hands. Of course, now we live in much more enlightened times, but back in the 1980s, even though medical science was clear that HIV couldn't be transmitted by touch, not many were willing to take the risk.

Perhaps this is something of the frisson of horror and delight which onlookers experienced when they watched this exchange between Jesus and the woman with the discharge of blood. In the Old Testament, uncleanness was contagious. This is not to suggest that there was any sense of germ theory behind, say, the leprosy laws, but nonetheless the uncleanness could be transmitted from person to person or object.

Leviticus 15 has two such examples of the transmission of uncleanness.

The first half of the chapter is a set of laws about the uncleanness of a man with a discharge, and the second half is a parallel account of the uncleanness surrounding a woman with an abnormal discharge. In our modern environment, where biblical menstrual uncleanness is invoked as an example of patriarchy and female oppression, it is worth noting the balance here.

However, we will focus on the female half of the chapter, because of its relevance to the gospel story. Notice that the uncleanness can be transmitted in a number of steps. Contact with the unclean woman will make bedding and seating unclean (v. 26). Contact with those unclean linens or cushions will make another person unclean (v. 27). One assumes that that person could also transmit their uncleanness to another person. Once again, let us recall, this is not ancient germ theory. This is about categories of thought that are alien to our 21st-century worldview.

The important thing to note, though, is that when the unclean woman touches Jesus – and the gospel writer has used the word 'touch' (*hapto*) four times in the account, least we overlook it – the process works in reverse. Jesus is not made unclean by the encounter; the woman is made clean. As Marcus Borg puts it, 'In the teaching of Jesus, holiness, not uncleanness, was understood to be contagious' (Borg, *Conflict, Holiness and Politics in the Teachings of Jesus: Studies in the Bible and early Christianity*, Trinity Press International, 1998, p. 147).

3 Even the Samaritan

Luke 10:25–37

The origins of the Samaritans are obscure. Dig through the ancient writings on the subject and you will find accounts highly coloured by the writer's own ideology. The Samaritan literature traces Samaritan origins back to the time of Eli, and asserts that the Samaritans were the true descendants of Israel who remained faithful when the rest of the nation tolerated the move of the cultic centre from Gerizim to Shiloh and then to Jerusalem. Unsurprisingly, the Jewish account of the situation was different and traced Samaritans back to the mixed race of people that ensued after the deliberate colonisation of Israel by Assyria (2 Kings 17:24–41). This was elaborated by Josephus, who described how Sanballat built a sanctuary on Mount Gerizim for his son-in-law, the priest Manasseh, who had been expelled from Jerusalem.

Whatever the accuracy of these accounts, history is clear that in 112 or 111BC, the Hasmonean priest John Hyrcanus burned an existing temple on Mount Gerizim. This helps explain the hostility between Jews and Samaritans by the time of Jesus and also the dichotomy expressed by the Samaritan woman (John 4:20).

This hostile environment is apparent in the background of the gospel accounts. The lawyer cannot even bear to name as Samaritan the fictional character whose actions honesty compels him to endorse (Luke 10:37). On another occasion, Jesus was rejected from a Samaritan village because of his onward destination to Jerusalem: 'He sent messengers ahead of him, who went and entered a village of the Samaritans, to make preparations for him. But the people did not receive him, because his face was set towards Jerusalem' (Luke 9:52–53). And some of Jesus' critics seem to think that being a Samaritan and having a demon were pretty much synonymous (John 8:48)!

In a striking challenge to this hostile environment, Jesus has a prolonged conversation with a Samaritan woman (John 4:7–42) and instructs his disciples to take the gospel to Samaria as the first step of world evangelisation (Acts 1:8). And, of course, in answer to the question, 'Who is my neighbour?', he tells the tale of the good Samaritan. But we must be careful not to allow familiarity to blunt the cutting edge of this story for us. What is so striking about Jesus' parable is that the Samaritan was not the victim who needed help, but the helper who was to be emulated. Jesus simultaneously challenges the norm of othering the out-group and turns the tables on in-group ethical superiority. This is not the only place where Jesus does such a thing. See, for example, Luke 11:29–32 and Matthew 11:20–24. No wonder he was so unpopular with the in-group authorities.

4 Welcoming angels and doing it for the Lord

Genesis 18:1–19

This story of Abraham's hospitality is often regarded as the archetypal example of hospitality in the Jewish and Christian writings. For example, it is reflected in the rabbinical writings of the Babylonian Talmud, where the Testament of Abraham (20:15) says, 'Let us too, my beloved brothers, imitate the hospitality of the patriarch Abraham.'

The account reflects many of the features of ancient Near-Eastern hospitality. It is, essentially, a carefully choreographed set of protocols to manage the potentially hostile threat that exists between strangers who meet. The essential elements which are demonstrable in this story are: the traveller is an unexpected stranger; he does not actively request hospitality but makes his presence known; a modest offer of hospitality is made, which is exceeded by the meal which follows ('a morsel of bread… a calf, tender and good', vv. 5, 7); a time limit is stated ('refresh yourselves, and after that you may pass on', v. 5); the hospitality is free; there is social interaction and the parties are no longer strangers ('I will surely return to you about this time next year', v. 10); the host accompanies the departing guests on the first stage of their journey. Many of these elements can also be found in other stories of biblical hospitality, such as Genesis 19:1–11; 24:15–61; 29:1–11; Exodus 2:15–22; Judges 19.

Of course, what is unusual about this story is that Abraham is not hosting travelling nomads, but God himself (or perhaps God plus two angels – the exact interpretation of who these figures are is disputed). This story is almost certainly what the writer to the Hebrews has in view when he or she writes, 'Do not neglect to show hospitality to strangers, for by doing that some have entertained angels without knowing it' (Hebrews 13:2, NRSV).

But perhaps we are not to regard this as unusual at all. By definition, we will not realise if we are unknowingly hosting angels, but the words of Jesus help us to realise that when we serve the stranger, we are always serving the Lord: '"Lord, when did we see you hungry and feed you, or thirsty and give you drink?"… And the King will answer them, "Truly, I say to you, as you did it to one of the least of these my brothers, you did it to me"' (Matthew 25:37, 40).

5 Journeying hospitality

Luke 15:11–32

Another thing that is striking about the Abraham story considered in the previous reflection is the way that the hospitality relationship becomes inverted as the strangers assume the dominant role and entrust Abraham with divine knowledge. Such inversion of the host-guest relationship is apparent in many of the meals that Jesus shared. So, for example, he was invited to Zacchaeus' house but later declared, 'Today salvation has come to this house' (Luke 19:9). At the wedding of Cana in Galilee (John 2:1–12), he arrived as a guest but ended up being the provider of many litres of wine. And, in perhaps the supreme example, on Resurrection Sunday he was the guest in Emmaus of two despondent disciples, and yet as he broke the bread with them, by this richly symbolic act he summoned them into fellowship with him (Luke 24:13–30).

This is one of the ways in which Jesus challenges our understanding of hospitality. We might typically imagine the host remaining at home, preparing a meal and welcoming the arriving guest into their own space. But being host in another's home is a different order of hospitality. It is an example of travelling welcome, of hospitality that does not wait for the guest but seeks them out.

The story of the prodigal son is essentially a story of divine welcome, at least inasmuch as it deals with the father and the younger son. The father's reacceptance of his son is demonstrated by his active movement towards the prodigal, an action which in the ancient world of its setting was highly remarkable:

The word run in Greek (dramōn) is the technical term used for the footraces in the stadium … 'His father saw him and had compassion and raced.' It is not just a slow shuffle or a fast walk – he races! In the Middle East a man of his age and position always walks in a slow, dignified fashion. It is safe to assume that he has not run anywhere for any purpose for forty years.

Kenneth Bailey, *The Cross and the Prodigal: Luke 15 through the eyes of Middle Eastern peasants* (InterVarsity Press, 2010), p. 67

The hospitality of the Christ-event is a journey of the Son to the earth 'while we still were sinners' (Romans 5:8). This downward trajectory is highlighted by Paul's stepwise description of Jesus' humiliation in Philippians 2:6–8. The New Testament description of divine hospitality is characterised by its active movement, not its passive receptivity.

6 Hospitality in the context of need

Luke 7:36–50

We have already considered how in Jesus the roles of guest and host become intertwined. But there is a further element to this complexity to explore. In the life of Jesus there is no act of generosity which is not positioned within the context of his own need; nor is there a moment of need which lacks an expression of generosity from him. Indeed, his life and teaching suggest that the two are inextricable.

Jesus is frequently portrayed as being in need and permitting others to care for him. He was supported by the private means of wealthy women (Luke 8:2–3). He had nowhere to lay his head (Luke 9:58), or he was the guest of friends (Mark 11:11; compare John 12:1–2). In today's reading, we see him allowing the sinful woman to minister to his feet. But it is clear that, even while beholden to others, he always demonstrated generosity. At both the feeding of the five thousand and of the four thousand, Jesus was the recipient of someone else's hospitality (John 6:9; Mark 8:5), before hosting a picnic for a multitude. He asked the Samaritan woman at the well for a drink (John 4:6–7) before speaking to her of living water. Each of these incidents constitutes a blurring of the distinction between guest and host, where, by means of receiving a service from others, often from the out-group, he flouted societal conventions to witness to the radical inclusion of the kingdom of God.

And Jesus established this pattern of generous acceptance of generous hospitality as a pattern for mission: 'Carry no money bag, no knapsack, no sandals, and greet no one on the road. Whatever house you enter, first say, "Peace be to this house!" And if a son of peace is there, your peace will rest upon him. But if not, it will return to you. And remain in the same house, eating and drinking what they provide, for the labourer deserves his wages' (Luke 10:4–7).

The most striking instance of Jesus' neediness and hospitality is, of course, found at the cross, itself the paramount act of self-donation, resulting in the most utter privation. And yet even here, generosity and hospitality find expression: 'Truly, I say to you, today you will be with me in Paradise' (Luke 23:43); 'Woman, behold, your son… Behold, your mother' (John 19:26–27).

Guidelines

In ancient Israel, the concept of 'world' was limited to a few nations in the Middle East, and the distribution of those whose needs one might actually know and be able to meet was much more limited than that. Today, our computer newsfeeds and television screens beam us images of the needy from all over the world; we are in continual danger of compassion fatigue, and we can feel genuinely overwhelmed by the enormity of global need and our own limitations. Further, we might ask what the limits of our responsibility are towards those we identify as neighbour. Are we obliged to see that they don't starve? That they can access education? That they can enjoy the same lifestyle as us? Where does loving our neighbour begin and end?

Writing many centuries ago, Thomas Aquinas offers advice on the matter. He argues that there is a hierarchy in terms of the love we owe to others (*ordo amoris*). This hierarchy relates to the proximity and the number of ways in which we are able to love them: 'We love more those who are more nearly connected with us, since we love them in more ways,' and, 'One's obligation to love a person is proportionate to the gravity of the sin one commits in acting against that love' (Thomas Aquinas, *Summa Theologica*, II-II, q. 26, a. 6–7). Is this a useful way to approach the problem? If so, how might this be worked out in our society?

FURTHER READING

Luke Bretherton, *Hospitality as Holiness: Christian witness amid moral diversity* (Ashgate, 2006).

Elizabeth Newman, *Untamed Hospitality: Welcoming God and other strangers* (Brazos Press, 2007).

Helen Paynter, '"Love the sojourner": the Old Testament ethic of hospitality', *Baptist Ministers' Journal*, October 2016 (vol. 332), 9–15.

Helen Paynter, 'The ethics of jubilee in Leviticus 25', *Ministry Today*, March 2016: **ministrytoday.org.uk/magazine/issues/66/505**.

Helen Paynter, '"Make yourself at home": the tensions and paradoxes of hospitality in dialogue with the Bible', *The Bible and Critical Theory* 14.1 (2018).

Christine D. Pohl, *Making Room: Recovering hospitality as a Christian tradition* (Eerdmans, 1999).

Miroslav Volf, *Exclusion and Embrace: A theological exploration of identity, otherness, and reconciliation* (Abingdon, 1996).

Matthew 3—7

Andy Angel

Matthew continues his gospel of Jesus the Messiah and Son of God. In his prologue to the narratives of Jesus' birth and early life, Matthew has underlined the fact that Jesus is the Messiah and Son of David. Through these stories and their fulfilment of prophecy, Matthew has shown the gospel audience that Jesus is Emmanuel, God with us, the one who will save God's people from their sins, the prince who will shepherd God's people Israel, and the Son of God.

We now meet the adult Jesus. John the Baptist introduces him as the one who will winnow and judge. Throughout the gospel Jesus talks of the day he comes to judge. He will establish justice and that will involve rewarding the righteous and punishing sinners. However, Jesus also comes to winnow – to sort out the wheat from the chaff – to teach the ways of God and to call people to repentance and lives of discipleship. He does this by explaining how God calls us to live and by helping people to live this way. We have one of the fullest collections of Jesus' teaching on how we should live in this series of studies in the sermon on the mount. As the closing parable of the sermon makes clear, Jesus does not call us to understand or have a healthy critical appreciation of his teaching, but to live it out.

However, Jesus doesn't simply describe how we should live and then leave us to get on with it. He walks alongside his disciples. Present with us every day, he teaches us how to live as we listen to his words and look to him in prayer. As we pray and listen to him in prayer and Bible reading, the living Jesus shows us how to move forwards in our lives – in even the trickiest situations. In the gospel story, he also lived out his teaching as an example to all of us down the years of how to live. This is one of the central themes of the gospel of Matthew: Jesus as the obedient Son of God. Jesus calls us all to live out his teaching as part of our mission to teach the nations to obey all that Jesus has commanded us. Jesus also commits to doing this work in us and through us, present with us every day until he comes again, having shown us the way by his own example here among us.

Unless otherwise stated, Bible quotations are my own translation.

1 Preaching a fuller Jesus

Matthew 3:1–12

I want to change the question: not 'What would Jesus do?' but 'What does Jesus do?' and 'What will Jesus do?' In preaching his fiery words, John the Baptist paints a picture of Jesus' ministry which actually sets the scene for the rest of the gospel. He describes Jesus as the one who 'will baptise you with the Holy Spirit and with fire' (v. 11), which finds its place in many contemporary churches that enjoy the presence, ministry and gifts of the Holy Spirit. However, unlike some of these churches, John does not stop there.

John continues with the following words: 'his winnowing fork is in his hand, and he will thoroughly clean up the threshing floor. He will gather up the wheat in his storehouse and he will burn up the chaff with unquenchable fire' (v. 12). Enter the adult Jesus into the gospel narrative. No longer the baby of a refugee family in the infancy stories, but the person who is about to enact the judgement of God. Israel is compared to a threshing floor that is in a mess. It needs sorting out. Someone must come in with the requisite tools to sort the good from the bad – so the good can be kept and the bad can be destroyed. The image Matthew puts on John's lips to announce the entrance of the adult Jesus is arresting.

Jesus comes to thoroughly clean up the people of God. John warns people to be ready. The Pharisees were looking for a renewal of holiness in the nation. Some were clearly not living up to their own hope: John tells them to 'bear fruit worthy of repentance' and not to think they can rely on the promises of God to Abraham and his descendants without living out their faith in obedience (vv. 8–9). Stark words to those who thought they were on the right path. What hope would there be for the unholy? 'Repent' (v. 2) or turn away from your sins. First, ask forgiveness. Then, live holy (not sinful) lives.

To any of us who have grown comfortable with the idea that we can rely on the promises of God and do not really need to do anything else, John's picture will hopefully shake us up. God does love, call and forgive – but he changes us so that we live changed lives, not return to our old ones.

2 The obedient Son

The first action of the man with the winnowing fork is confusing. He comes to John to be baptised. John the Baptist was as confused as we are: '*I need to be baptised by you*, and you come to me?' (v. 14). John seems all too aware of who was really holy. But Jesus tells John to leave it because 'it makes sense for us to fulfil all righteousness' (v. 15). John seems to have understood, as he then baptised Jesus.

We, however, can feel rather left in the dark. The meaning of Jesus' words is disputed, but there are clues. When John objects, Jesus does not respond that he needs forgiveness of sins; his baptism is not about cleansing sin. Jesus talks about John baptising him as being fitting for both of them. John was God's prophet, calling all who were willing to baptism so that they became one of God's renewed people. So Jesus gets baptised to enter this renewed people alongside everyone else. If he is to lead people in obedience to God, he too must be obedient. The one with the winnowing fork comes alongside those he comes to winnow and lives the life he comes to teach others to live.

Then comes the apocalyptic moment. Apocalyptic moments are when the heavens are opened and God reveals their mysteries. Their mysteries are God's next steps to save and judge his creation. The Spirit pours out on Jesus in a form reminiscent of God's judgement and forgiveness in the story of Noah (Genesis 6—9). God announces that Jesus is his Son in words reminiscent of Psalm 2:7, which continue, 'Ask of me, and I will make the nations your heritage… You shall break them with a rod of iron' (Psalm 2:8–9). God's words remind us of Jesus' commission to make disciples of all nations before he comes again to judge (Matthew 28:18–20). Commissioning Jesus is the next (and greatest) step in God's plan to save the world and prepare it for the day of judgement.

God commissioned Jesus to make the nations his heritage and Jesus continues that mission through his church today – calling people from sin and to God in baptism, and teaching them to obey all Jesus has commanded. As the obedient Son of his heavenly Father, Jesus continues that mission with, in and through us his disciples today.

3 Real sons and daughters

Matthew 4:1–11

Jesus has shown himself to be the obedient Son of God in baptism. God has declared Jesus his Son and that he is delighted with him (3:17). In doing so, God has commissioned Jesus to make the nations his heritage and establish his justice among them. Then the Spirit leads Jesus into the desert to be tempted by the devil. Jesus fasts.

The devil seeks to steer Jesus off course from being the obedient Son by telling him to stop fasting and to make bread to eat (v. 3). Maybe a hungry Jesus might give up fasting, just as the children of Israel had murmured against God in the desert when they were hungry (Exodus 16; Numbers 11). Jesus responds from scripture (Deuteronomy 8:3) that we do not live simply from food but from every word from the mouth of God.

Noting that Jesus responds from scripture to affirm his commitment to obedience, the devil plays the same game in reverse. He uses scripture (Psalm 91:11) to try to put Jesus in a situation where he forces God to act for his protection rather that obediently following where God leads. Again, Jesus responds from the law (Deuteronomy 6:16) that obedient sons do not put God to the test.

Finally, the devil tries to tempt Jesus by offering him the result of the ministry to which God has called him: authority over all the nations of the world. He can get this by worshipping Satan. Once more Jesus quotes the law (Deuteronomy 6:13) that you shall worship and serve the Lord God alone. Jesus bids Satan depart, and Satan does so.

Satan sought to wreck the ministry of Jesus by attacking him right at the point of his calling: 'If you are the Son of God…' God has called Jesus his Son, so Satan tries to reshape what sonship means. However, Jesus remains committed to fasting and feeding on the word of God. He uses scripture to listen to God rather that telling God what to do. He recognises that following God and accepting his ministry can only find true fulfilment in obedience to God – however glamorous alternative paths to glory may seem. Jesus remains firm in his obedience to the Father. In this, he sets us all an example of what obedient sons and daughters of the heavenly Father do. All of us are called to follow God and live out our faith in our daily lives (whether we are a minister, a homemaker, in business or anything else). The question is: how do we respond?

4 Ministry under threat

The obedient Son has faced a heavenly threat. Now he faces an earthly one. He was associated with John the Baptist, but now John has been arrested, so Jesus withdraws to Galilee (v. 12). Jesus knows that John's arrest means he also may be under threat. However, he does not withdraw from ministry. Quite the opposite, he enters public ministry. He sets up his base in Capernaum in a way that Matthew sees as the fulfilment of prophecy (vv. 14–16).

Matthew notes that the location (region of Zebulun and Naphtali, beside the sea, v. 13) is exactly as in the prophecy (v. 14; compare Isaiah 8:23—9:1). Jesus has become the great light that has arisen over the peoples who have been living in darkness and the shadow of death. Matthew sees a great day dawning. In calling the region 'Galilee *of the Gentiles*' (v. 15), Matthew has chosen a prophetic word which speaks of Jesus' calling to bring God's salvation and justice to all the nations.

Jesus continues the ministry of John. His proclamation uses exactly John's words: 'Repent, for the kingdom of heaven has drawn near' (v. 17; compare 3:2). Note that Jesus does not say 'reform' or 'receive'. Many today think that the kingdom means the transformation of society. Surely if Jesus had meant this, he would have said 'reform' or 'rebel'. Many others think the kingdom consists of God doing miracles to heal and restore. If this was all there was to the kingdom, then surely Jesus would have said 'receive'. But he did not. Jesus said 'repent'.

The idea of the kingdom of heaven goes back to hymns celebrating God's kingship (e.g. Psalms 97 and 99) in which God comes to the earth to judge. When he does this, he establishes justice by rewarding his righteous people and punishing the wicked among his people and the Gentiles. Through these actions, he establishes peace and justice among his people and throughout the world.

The kingdom of heaven starts with the judgement of God. That is why Jesus called people to repent – rather than to reform or receive or anything else. He wants people to enter his kingdom, and they cannot do so unless they are righteous. Sometimes we lose this focus in our churches. Perhaps it is time to kiss goodbye to some of our notions of the kingdom of heaven and refocus on the words and teaching of Jesus.

5 Calling disciples

Sometimes an author uses details of time or place to send a message to their audience. Matthew does that here. In the immediately preceding scene (4:12–17), he has Jesus move to Galilee beside the sea, where his ministry as a great light dawning on the Gentiles begins. Here, he sets the scene of the calling of the first disciples 'beside the Sea of Galilee' (v. 18). This being the place of the light dawning, Jesus' commitment to make them fishers of people places their call right in the centre of his mission to bring God's justice and salvation to the whole earth.

Matthew uses a word twice in this story that he has not yet used in the gospel and does not use more than once anywhere else in such a short space: 'immediately' (vv. 20, 22). When Peter and Andrew hear Jesus' call, they leave their nets immediately (v. 20). When James and John hear his call, they leave their boat and father immediately (v. 22). They leave work and family behind and follow Jesus. Matthew uses the scene to model true discipleship. This involves total commitment to Jesus. As Jesus says later in the gospel, 'Whoever loves father or mother more than me is not worthy of me… and whoever does not take up their cross and follow me is not worthy of me' (10:37–38).

The calling also foreshadows the final scene of the gospel, where Jesus commissions these same disciples (and others) to go out and make disciples of all the nations, baptising them and teaching them to obey everything Jesus has commanded (28:18–20). However, before he can make them fishers of all the Gentile nations, Jesus has a lot to teach them and spends much of the gospel mentoring them.

For all of us who call ourselves disciples, this raises at least two questions: how total is my commitment – am I willing to give up time, work, leisure, money and so on to follow where Jesus leads me? And, what do I need to learn to minister his gospel? We are all called to make disciples, bringing people to faith and teaching each other obedience to all Jesus commands. What do I need to learn so that I can be more faithful in this calling?

6 Ministry

Jesus continues his public ministry. Various details catch the eye and imagination. Matthew says that Jesus teaches 'in *their* synagogues' (v. 23). These were the places where many Jews met to listen to and study the law each sabbath. Jesus was joining their gatherings and teaching them the law. The obedient Son was teaching his Father's people what obedience to their heavenly Father looked like. However, he was doing so on *their* ground, and the way Matthew puts this right at the start of Jesus' ministry hints at the rejection he suffers as he moves towards Jerusalem and the cross. However, his commitment to teaching people how to live as obedient disciples, even in the face of threat, is noteworthy. As a result, we must ask ourselves how strong our commitment to learning how to live as obedient disciples is.

Matthew also talks of Jesus preaching 'the good news of the kingdom' (v. 23). Given that Jesus calls people to repent, he envisages that God will come to judge. So why 'good news'? First, when God judges, he restores the righteous and brings the promised blessing to his people. This is surely good news. Second, who does not yearn for justice? When God judges, he brings justice. This is also good news. The only sting in the tail is when our sins deserve punishment so that justice might be done. However, there is also good news here. True repentance is met by forgiveness and the door opened to new life. If we truly repent, we turn from unjust ways to just ways of behaving. So not only do we receive God's blessing when he comes to judge but also, in the meantime, we live in ways that bless others. Is there anything in my life that needs changing so that I might live more justly? For example, do my purchases support fair working practices?

Finally, Jesus' ministry is marked by his extraordinary power to heal 'every sickness and every disease among the people' (v. 23). The picture of the gossip spreading and everyone who was ill, tormented, demon-possessed, lunatic or paralytic coming to him remains startling. Many of us who have experienced the remarkable healing power of God read such words with longing: come, Lord Jesus, in mighty power and do these same works again today.

Guidelines

Matthew gives the adult Jesus a remarkable entrance to the gospel: with a winnowing fork in his hand to clean up the mess of unrighteous Israel. The righteous will be gathered into God's people and the unrighteous destroyed. So Jesus proclaims, 'the kingdom of heaven is at hand' (4:17). In the face of coming judgement, he calls people to repentance. As he does this, he teaches them the ways of God and heals their diseases. His ministry is the long-prophesied light dawning on the whole world.

This ought to make us think about the way we do church today. In the parts of the UK where I have ministered, we focus on what will bring people into church and part of that has increasingly involved soft-pedalling over the challenges of faith. Jesus does the exact opposite. He focuses on what will bring people into the kingdom of heaven and presents them with the starkest challenge of all: 'repent', that is, put everything sinful that stands between yourself and God on the table, ask forgiveness for it and turn away from it forever. Then live in the ways of righteousness and justice that Jesus teaches. This seems a tall order, but it is the foundation and central focus of Jesus' ministry. Matthew begins to expound what that looks like in the next section of the gospel – the sermon on the mount.

Matthew will teach us more about what Jesus teaches and the way he teaches his people as the chapters of the gospel unfold. However, in these opening scenes of Jesus' adult ministry, there is much for us to chew over today. I was once in a ministerial training group where the facilitator asked how many in the room had preached on the judgement of God in the last three years: out of about 45 people, two raised their hands. Do we present the reality of the coming judgement to people in our witness to Jesus as disciples called to make disciples? If so, great. Ask Jesus how we can become more effective. If not, pray. Ask him for the courage to speak out and to deal with whatever it is in our characters that blocks us from doing this, so that we can do so naturally and with love – because surely this is a fundamental part of our calling in Christ.

1 The beatitudes

Matthew 5:2–10

Matthew begins his task of recording what Jesus teaches about discipleship. In this famous sermon on the mount, we hear how Jesus calls his disciples to live. However, Jesus begins by pronouncing blessings on those who are properly disposed towards God. They are not instructions in disguise, but they do give an indication of the kind of person God will bless. So if we seek God's blessing, it makes a great deal of sense to ask him in our repentance to take from us everything that prevents us from being this kind of person.

Children's activity books often include spot-the-difference puzzles. It is worth doing a similar exercise between Jesus' blessings in verses 3–12 and Isaiah 61, as Jesus echoes many of the words and ideas of this prophecy in the beatitudes. The people in Isaiah 61 sit in the ruins of Jerusalem, desperate for God to act. They find themselves entirely reliant and dependent on God. They long to see God demonstrate his glory by restoring his people. They weep in the ruins of Jerusalem.

Jesus claims that God will bless those with this kind of spirituality: who long to see justice done and God's people living in purity and holiness of lives – 'those who hunger and thirst for righteousness' (v. 6). Such people mourn for the lack of obedience to God among his people (v. 4) and so are broken in spirit (v. 3). However, their approach to the restoration of God's people involves no anger, reproach, accusation or sarcasm. Instead, they are humble, meek and merciful, and they make for peace. These people are pure in heart and mind. Let each one of us pray that God establishes (or continues to nurture) such a spirituality in us. As Jesus promises in the first and last of these blessings, if this is who we are, then God will surely bless us with the everlasting joy of life in the kingdom of heaven when Jesus comes to judge.

2 Light and law

Jesus turns from pronouncing blessings to talking directly to his disciples in verse 12 and continues like this until near the end of the sermon. He tells his disciples to rejoice in persecution, because God will reward them for their faithfulness (vv. 11–12). As salt and light in the world, they are to remain distinctive so that others 'will see your good works and glorify your Father in heaven' (v. 16).

But obedient witness is costly. Our righteousness must exceed that of the scribes and Pharisees or we will not enter the kingdom of heaven (v. 20). This rather tall order can lead us to despair, so some people think that Jesus is just setting up some kind of impossible gold standard so we all realise that we need his forgiveness. They say that he does not really mean that we need to obey his teachings. We just need to see we cannot meet the standard and repent. But this is unlikely, as Jesus is talking with people who have already repented. And the closing sections of this sermon show that Jesus expects us to take his teaching on how to behave seriously.

But there is a note of encouragement in the seemingly stiff strictures of verses 17–20. Having said that he has not come to destroy the law or the prophets, Jesus says, 'I have come not to destroy but to fulfil' (v. 17). Jesus did not say that he had come to check whether *we* were fulfilling or destroying the law and the prophets by our behaviour. He says that *he* has come to fulfil them. In placing this right at the start of Jesus' interpretation of the law and teaching on how to live, Matthew drops a hint at the answer to our problem when faced with these great teachings and our sinful lack of desire to practise them.

Jesus really is the answer. He will fulfil the teaching of the law and prophets in us. He will enable us to live out his teachings. He develops this later in the gospel when he calls us all to learn from him (11:29) and when he promises to be with us in our mission of teaching the nations to obey all he has commanded (28:20). The man with the winnowing fork who comes to sort the wheat from the chaff is willing to walk alongside chaff and help it become wheat. As the old song says, 'Trust and obey, for there is no other way to be happy in Jesus…'

3 Adultery

Jesus now turns to interpreting specific commands in the law: 'do not murder' (v. 21, compare Exodus 20:13; Deuteronomy 5:17) and 'do not commit adultery' (v. 27, compare Exodus 20:14; Deuteronomy 5:18). I would like to focus on Jesus' teaching on adultery as, in at least my experience, this text has sometimes been abused to place joyless, unhealthy and utterly unnecessary strictures on our sexuality.

Anyone who has read the Song of Solomon must realise that scripture celebrates human sexuality. (Even if someone interprets it as being about our relationship with God, it still uses erotic imagery positively.) Commonly, verse 28 seems to be used to condemn the sex drive as it is frequently mis-interpreted as saying 'if anyone looks at woman with desire for her', which would constitute a blanket condemnation of at least the male sex drive. However, it does not say this. The command being interpreted is to not commit adultery. Therefore, the context clearly implies that the 'anyone' here is a married man. The Greek of the next few words clearly expresses desire and intention and is best translated 'looking at a woman in order to lust after her'. Again, the context is adultery, so the woman can hardly be his wife. She must be another woman. The action Jesus condemns is delib-erately nurturing an attraction for someone who is not one's own wife. As a good Jew who recognised that God made us 'male and female' for sex and marriage (Matthew 19:3–9), Jesus would hardly condemn women and men for being sexually attracted to each other.

Then Jesus tells men to cut out their right eye and cut off their right hand if they cause them to sin. Why only the right, when most men use both eyes to act on their lust? Probably because it makes a nice parallel with the right hand (v. 30). Deliberately nurturing lust, following up the lust with the eye(s) and then with the right hand suggest that Jesus is talking pretty plainly to the men in his audience: do not act out your lust visually or in masturbation (a parallel Jewish text in Babylonian Talmud tractate Niddah 13a–b justi-fies this line of interpretation). Again, this is no blanket condemnation of sexual attraction or masturbation. What Jesus condemns here is cheating on one's spouse in the mind and in acting this out. His vision for the inti-macy of marriage is wonderfully romantic. In contemporary culture (just as for churches reading these words in ancient Greek and Roman culture), this clearly speaks against the use of pornography to act out lustful desires. Jesus desires that we experience our God-given sexuality in healthy ways that fulfil others as well as ourselves.

4 Making commitments

Matthew 5:31–37

Jesus now turns to interpreting laws around two different commitments: marriage and vows. I will not focus on Jesus' teaching on divorce and remarriage (compare Deuteronomy 24:1–4) as this is better done when interpreting Matthew 19, where Jesus gives a much fuller explanation of his thinking. Rather, I will focus on making vows, which seems to get less attention in church teaching programmes.

First, the words that Jesus cites – 'do not swear falsely but fulfil your oaths for the Lord's sake' (v. 33) – can only refer to the kind of oaths in which people promise to do something for God (e.g. those found in Leviticus 19:12; Numbers 30:3–15; Deuteronomy 23:21–23). They cannot refer to the making of oaths to prove innocence (e.g. Exodus 22:10–11; Numbers 5:19–22) as these oaths leave the oath-taker nothing to fulfil. Jesus is talking about promissory oaths in this text. (Incidentally, oaths to prove innocence are the only ones which people are commanded to make under certain circumstances. Jesus' condemnation of oaths in verse 34 does not concern these oaths but promissory oaths. So, Jesus does not contradict the law here, as the law never commands that anyone should make a promissory oath under particular circumstances.)

Jesus' concern about taking promissory oaths is that it dishonours God. Here, he fully agrees with the teaching of the law. The commandments cited above on taking these oaths instruct people to fulfil their oaths so as to avoid dishonouring God. Deuteronomy 23:22 instructs refraining from taking oaths if you are not going to keep them. Jesus simply makes the same point with greater strength. In order not to dishonour God or anything in his creation, do not make promissory oaths. Just say 'yes' or 'no'. Jesus' teaching here really ought to get us thinking not simply about vain commitments we might make but about the truthfulness and integrity of our speech generally. Honest speech honours God. Dishonest speech comes from the evil one.

5 True love

In his final two interpretations of words of the law, Jesus tackles 'an eye for an eye and a tooth for a tooth' (Exodus 21:24; Leviticus 24:20; Deuteronomy 19:21) and 'you shall love your neighbour' (Leviticus 19:18), to which is added 'and hate your enemy', a phrase that is found nowhere in the law. Both these sections focus on the outrageous love of God, who in many ways blesses both the righteous and the unrighteous as an example to us – to love both those who love us and those who do not.

Jesus' exploration of 'an eye for an eye' is fascinating. The law uses this idea as a principle of justice (Leviticus 24:10–23), both as proportionate punishment in retributive justice (Deuteronomy 19:21) and as a principle for punishment which underlies paying compensation (Exodus 21:22–27). Jesus charges his disciples not to quote this principle for justice in a mean-minded way but to work out how they can bless evildoers. If someone slaps you on the right cheek, offer the left. If someone is taking you to court to sue you for your outer garments, give them your underwear too. As well as using outrageous humour, Jesus points out that even when we are being wronged and at our most defensive, we ought to be thinking of how we can bless the other. Given the Jewish anger at Roman military oppression and collusion with local governments, the idea that if a soldier commandeered you into carrying their pack a mile, you should offer to do it for two, must have stung. Jesus cuts right to the heart of our anger, resentments and unwillingness to show generosity to others, and teaches us that this is precisely the place where he wants generosity shown. Give freely and do not refuse the one who wants to borrow.

As with all his interpretations of these commands and words from the law in this chapter of Matthew, Jesus brings out (what he teaches is) the true meaning of these commands and the law. The law teaches great generosity: for example, to give generously to all in need (Deuteronomy 15:7–11) and to set free people who have sold themselves into slavery and set them up in life (Deuteronomy 15:12–28). God seeks in us the kind of generosity that goes above and beyond what people do in the cultures around us.

6 Almsgiving and fasting

The most striking thing about Jesus' teaching about almsgiving and fasting is that Jesus does not say 'if you give alms…' or 'if you fast…' but 'whenever you…' (vv. 2, 16). For Jesus, these are basic spiritual disciplines which he expects of those who follow him. Jesus expects us to give to the poor out of our love and generosity towards others – on which he has already taught (Matthew 5:38–48). He expects us not simply to pray but to fast also.

We are all aware of Jesus' teaching that we should do what we do for God without making a song and dance about it. However, sometimes I wonder whether we are quite aware of the generosity and commitment that Jesus requires of us. Take giving alms, for example. Jesus teaches later in this gospel that people should tithe (as well as observe the weightier matters of the law like justice, mercy and faithfulness; Matthew 23:23). That equals ten per cent of all income and production. Jesus teaches giving alms to the poor as well. That is a lot of personal wealth given to others. This would have been nothing new to Torah-observant Jews of Jesus' day. They were commanded to tithe all the produce of the field (Deuteronomy 14:22). They were also commanded to leave part of the crop for the poor to come and eat as they wanted (Leviticus 19:9–10; 23:22; Deuteronomy 24:19–22). Ancient Jews recognised that some people were poor on account of their own laziness or foolishness (Proverbs 6:10–11; 10:4; 14:23; 20:13; 23:20–21; 24:33–34; 28:19), but they were commanded to give nonetheless. God commanded generosity towards the poor whatever the reasons for their being poor.

Personally, I am challenged at the spirituality of Jesus' audience. They clearly fast and give alms. Bible teachers often criticise them, calling them hypocrites (as Jesus does) but I wonder if *we* have that right. For many of us, a little of this 'hypocrisy' might vastly improve our spiritual discipline. Do not get me wrong. I am not recommending that we repeat their mistakes, but I do think that we ought to get our own houses in order before we even think of picking up the first stone.

Guidelines

Jesus desires and requires that we live up to the most extraordinary standards. No other rabbi ever legislated for how his listeners were to think or feel. They legislated for how people were to behave. In the teachings we have looked at this week, Jesus does not simply tell us how to act but also how to feel and what to think about it. None of this teaching is easy.

Nor can we hide away in a kind of 1960s spiritual 'hippiedom' which says that Jesus claims that it is all about having the right attitude. Some have misinterpreted Jesus' words here to mean that Jesus thinks it is all about what is in our 'hearts' and getting strung up about obeying laws is 'legalism'. As soon as we get there, we begin to claim that actions do not matter provided the attitude is right. We then make out that we have the right and responsibility to decide what the right thing to do is, provided we do 'the loving thing'. But these myths have nothing to do with what Jesus says. Jesus does not disagree with the law at all in these verses. Jesus does not want people to murder, to commit adultery, to fail to give God what we have promised or to act unjustly, let alone to fail to love our friends. Jesus wants us to do all these things. He simply wants our attitudes to be right as well.

Jesus wants his people to hunger and thirst for righteousness – that is, to desire holiness so much that we ache for it. We are to be pure in heart and mind. Much as we long for his justice, our first thoughts in our relationships with others should be of mercy, kindness, gentleness and peace. We ought not only to live out justice but to go further, working out how we can show generosity, whether the recipients deserve it or not. This is a tall order, but it is not our work – it is the work of Jesus with us and in us.

1 Prayer

Matthew 6:5–15

One question people continue to ask about prayer is why we should bother with it. If God knows everything, we can hardly be telling him anything he does not know already. You might even say that Jesus thinks the same, as he says that God knows what we need before we ask (v. 8). However, Jesus' response to God's knowing everything is different. He assumes his disciples will pray ('whenever you pray…', v. 5), so he teaches us how to pray.

Before anything else, Jesus teaches us to pray that God's name will be made holy. This petition recalls Ezekiel 36:22–38, where God tells Israel that he is about to act to save them but not for their sake. He will act for the sake of his holy name. His people's sinful actions and idolatry have profaned his name among the peoples of the earth. Therefore, he will act to restore his great name so that the nations will realise that he is God when he displays his holiness before them. He displays his holiness by restoring his people. He cleanses them from their sins and puts a new spirit within them. He gives them a heart that is open to his will. He puts his spirit in his people so that they live out his commands.

When Jesus teaches us to pray 'hallowed by thy name', he reorders our minds and hearts. Rather than bringing our long list of petitions in prayer so that God does what we will, he teaches us to stand back and ask God to act to glorify himself among the nations so that they know that he is God. Rather than telling God how *we* want him to reshape our lives, we ask God how *he* wants to reshape our lives. We do ask God for what we need but we spend much more time asking God for forgiveness and committing to forgive others. We also focus on asking God to lead us out of the trials and temptations which might lead us to sin or give up our faith in him. Jesus refocuses our prayer, teaching us to pray for God's will to be done in our lives in the light of the day when his kingdom will come and he will judge the nations.

2 Money

Jesus gives us straight instruction on how we are to handle wealth and then offers us two parables to reflect on where we really are. The instruction is simple: do not store up wealth on earth but wealth in heaven. Jesus pictures those who follow him as receiving rewards in the kingdom of heaven (e.g. Matthew 19:29). In this age, wealth decays and can be stolen. The wealth of the age to come lasts forever. So where do we stand?

The first parable draws on the ancient Jewish understanding of the good and evil eye. When someone has a 'good eye', they are generous. Proverbs 22:9 literally translates as 'a good eye will be blessed because he gives his bread to the poor [or thin]'. The NRSV simply translates the first part of this verse as 'those who are generous are blessed', because the context makes it clear what 'good eye' means. So Jesus challenges his disciples: if you are generous, then you are living in God's will, but if you are mean with your money, then you are full of sin. The contrast is stark and so is the challenge.

The second parable draws on the ancient reality of slavery. Slaves were the property of another person. They had to do what they were instructed to do by their owners. Although there were slaves with more than one owner (e.g. Acts 16:16), the situation Jesus envisages points up an obvious problem – what do you do if different owners require contradictory things? But this picture does not simply ask whom we serve. It asks the equally poignant question of whether in reality we are in slavery to wealth. Are we free to be generous or are we tied to our money and property? Are we scared to let it go?

Jesus is interested in our hearts (v. 21), but we cannot make this a weak excuse for keeping our money to ourselves in the face of others' needs because we have a sentimental attachment to serving the poor in our imaginations. The heart is the will, the place we make our decisions. Every time we spend money, we tell God where our heart is.

3 Money worries

Matthew 6:25–34

'Because of this, I tell you, do not worry…' (v. 25). Jesus' opening words are startling. He has taught us that we are to be more generous than the hypocrites who give alms to the poor, which would be in addition to their tithes (6:2). He has just told us that we cannot serve God and money and that if we are not generous, our lives are full of sin and we are enslaved to money (6:22–24). Now he tells us not to worry. For any of us who find tithing difficult, let alone giving away money to the poor on top of this, Jesus' words are more than challenging.

However, Jesus leaves us no escape route from his words on the basis that he is some kind of utopian idealist. His final words on the topic demonstrate he knows the sobering nature of financial reality as most of us experience it: 'Do not worry about tomorrow because tomorrow will worry about itself; sufficient for the day is its own trouble' (v. 34). Jesus understands daily struggle. Indeed, he lived this out, having no income and surviving on the generosity of women who were in all likelihood dependent on others for their own ability to provide for Jesus and his disciples (Luke 8:1–3).

This is the place from which Jesus teaches us to look at the birds of the air and the lilies of the field. He starts from the place of worry (vv. 25, 28) and the lived experience of complete financial dependence on the generosity of others. But from this place, Jesus tells us to look to God.

We ought also to note that Jesus talks about God meeting the basic needs of food, drink and clothing. There were plenty of luxuries in the ancient world and Jesus knew all about them. He challenged one young man with many possessions to sell them and give the money to the poor (Matthew 19:20–22). However, Jesus does not promise his disciples great wealth – simply their basic needs – and he teaches his disciples to pray that God will give us our daily bread. Jesus does not pander to our selfish desires, but he does promise that God will meet our genuine needs. God's economy is generous and humble.

4 Handling difficulties with discernment

Matthew 7:1–12

Jesus instructs his disciples not to condemn so that they will not be condemned at the final judgement. He warns them that the measure with which they judge others will be the measure used to judge them. His warning cannot mean that we must refuse to engage in any kind of critical assessment of a difficult situation or relationship breakdown and how best we act upon it, as Jesus gives instructions to his disciples on exactly how we are to behave in such a situation (18:15–20). Rather, Jesus instructs us not to write each other off, unless we are willing for God to write us off on that great day.

He spells out one of the practicalities of this in the following parable. A splinter is a tiny part of a wooden beam. Jesus tells us not to try to take the splinter out of someone else's eye when we have a wooden beam in our own. If we struggle with a particular sin, we have no right to try to put this right in someone else's life – not least if our struggle is far greater than theirs. If we want to help others in some area of their life, then we first need to make sure that that area of our own lives is fully in order. Only then will we be in a position to help anybody with this aspect of life. As Jesus puts it: 'First take the beam out of your own eye and then you will see clearly enough to take the splinter out of your brother's eye' (v. 5). There is no place for hypocrisy in the ministry to which Jesus calls us.

Jesus' teaching here calls for humility and realism in the way we relate to and minister to each other. We ought to keep a careful check on ourselves so that we are aware of our capacities, our strengths and our shortcomings. We need (or need to develop) the humility and honesty which enable us to know where we can contribute something and where we best hold back and allow others to do what we are currently unable to do. Jesus does teach us to help each other get back on track, but he teaches us to do this in humility, grace, mercy and love.

5 Uncomfortable words

Matthew 7:13–20

Jesus now begins to close the sermon on the mount. His final words are all warnings. I can remember hearing many sermons on these sayings as a child. Taking the narrow path was a common theme back then. In the last few decades, the parts of the western church that I inhabit have grown less fond of the themes of judgement, obedience and the waywardness of the world. They seem to be swept under the carpet and replaced with talk about 'the kingdom'.

But these sayings are all about the kingdom. Jesus knows that the first thing God does to establish his kingdom is to judge – that is why he calls us to repent (4:17). He opened the sermon with a series of blessings which promised entry to the kingdom of heaven to those who are persecuted for the sake of righteousness (5:10). He has spent the greater part of the sermon explaining what righteousness looks like in practice and instructing his disciples to live this kind of life. Now, as he closes the sermon, he reminds us that just as there are rewards for those who follow him, there are also punishments for those who choose not to when he comes to judge.

Jesus warns us all that there are many more on the road to destruction than there are on the road to life, and he commands us to follow the narrow path. This means that our life and faith are likely to be countercultural. This is the reality for Christians in many parts of the world where faithful following of Jesus continues to stand out as different from the norm. In much of the west, we have been so keen to hold on to the links between church and wider society that we tend to accommodate ourselves to current trends in society. Too many of us today place the narrow road within the wider road of society to try to bridge the cultural gap. But this is to fail Jesus. Perhaps in the west, it is time to recognise that we have to choose Christ and his righteousness and that, in doing so, we will be outside the mainstream of society and this may well bring persecution. But those who are persecuted for the sake of righteousness inherit the kingdom.

6 The importance of being obedient

Matthew 7:21–29

Whenever I read these words, I am humbled. I aspire to have a ministry as effective as those of the people that Jesus turns away in verses 22–23. They have prophesied in his name, they have cast out demons in his name and they have worked many mighty miracles in his name. This kind of ministry not only fills many churches but during the last century has also created super-churches. So, when I think of my own ministry, I am awed by the remarkable nature of what these people have done in Jesus' name.

What could they have got so wrong that Jesus turns them away with the words 'I never knew you; depart from me, workers of lawlessness' (v. 23)? The answer is quite simply that they have not done the will of the Father (v. 21) but instead have lived unrighteous lives (v. 23) – that is, they have not lived out Jesus' teaching. On the day of judgement, Jesus will not be as impressed by our amazing ministries as we are. He is interested in something quite different: our obedience.

He brings this out in the following parable of the wise and foolish builders. The house that stands firm in the storm refers to the righteous life that will stand people in good stead on the day of judgement. The house that crashes in the storm refers to the disobedient life that will not survive the judgement of God. Interestingly, both builders heard the words of Jesus. The difference between them is not whether they heard his teaching. The difference is whether they put it into practice: 'Whoever hears these words *and does them* may be likened to a wise man…' (v. 24) and 'whoever hears these words and does not do them may be likened to a foolish man…' (v. 26). The words 'these words' refer back to all the teaching Jesus has given in the sermon on the mount on how we are to live. So Jesus finishes his sermon with this cautionary tale and he expects us to respond in action. He does not call us to know his words or to critically assess his words and form our own judgement on them; he calls us to live them out.

Guidelines

Matthew closes the sermon on the mount with some clear and stiff warnings from Jesus. We are not to take the easy route in life but are to walk the path of obedience to Jesus' teaching. We must be careful not to listen to people who teach another gospel, and we can work out pretty well whether they do so by the way they live. Are they living in obedience to Jesus' instruction? On that final day, they may be terribly impressed by their ministries, but Jesus will not accept them into the kingdom of heaven if they have not followed him as disciples, living his way. Jesus then turns to all of us to ask what the foundations of our own lives are, because only foundations of obedience will weather the storm of judgement day.

While we can read our way through the sayings of the sermon on the mount with a familiarity which breeds a cosy religious nostalgia, Jesus' words are actually rather challenging to most of us. They become increasingly uncomfortable the more our society puts moral choices before us. Obedience has become a dirty word in the contemporary west. Words like 'freedom', 'liberation', 'justice' and 'peace' have become the buzzwords of the western church. These are the kinds of things which people mean by 'the kingdom of God', and we seek it in our contemporary religious imagination and practice.

Jesus' teaching at the start of the gospel of Matthew challenges all this. He says blessed are the pure in heart, those who hunger and thirst for righteousness and those who are persecuted for righteousness – for they shall see the kingdom of heaven. Unless our righteousness exceeds that of the scribes and Pharisees, Jesus says we will not enter the kingdom of heaven. Jesus has a vision of our moral transformation and this lies right at the heart of the faith he teaches. This is good news for everyone else, as we will love them more in practice. And the good news for us is that Jesus himself does this work in us. He has come to fulfil the law and the prophets, because only he can. The obedient Son teaches each of us how to become obedient daughters and sons of our heavenly Father.

Seven words from the cross

David Spriggs

As part of our preparation for Holy Week and Good Friday, we will explore the so-called 'seven words from the cross'. These are short statements by Jesus recorded in the gospels as he endured the excruciating agony of crucifixion. Given that these are the last words of a dying man, and a man of supreme significance, it is understandable that they have been the focus for Christian devotion as well as expounded in many sermons and meditations.

Some of these 'words' can be considered prayers, because they are addressed to God; to listen in on these is a profound privilege. Some of them are spoken to people (e.g. to Jesus' mother and his beloved disciple, to the penitent thief) and indicate Jesus' capacity to transcend the most intense of pain as he expresses care and hope for them.

Although there is a received traditional order in which the words were spoken, we cannot be sure of this at all. This is because they are distributed across the gospels and most are unique to one gospel. We can be fairly certain that 'My God, my God, why have you forsaken me?' (Matthew 27:46; Mark 15:34) came several hours into the crucifixion, because we are given the time references for this. Others we can deduce must have come towards the end of his life, such as 'I am thirsty' and 'It is finished' (John 19:28, 30) and particularly 'Father, into your hands I commend my spirit' (Luke 23:46), as Luke adds, 'Having said this, he breathed his last.' We will follow the traditional order.

Although there is value in reflecting on these as a chain of sayings, we can also lose certain factors by abstracting them from the individual gospels. For instance, 'My God, my God, why have you forsaken me?' becomes even more breathtaking in Matthew and Mark, because it is the only saying attributed to Jesus. However, it seems likely that they have compressed the final hours of Jesus and there is a hint that it wasn't the only one.

Our primary focus will not be on historicity but on stimulating reflection for us today.

Unless otherwise stated, Bible quotations are from the New Revised Standard Version (Anglicised).

1 'Father, forgive them; for they do not know what they are doing'

Luke 23:32–38

Given the context of these words, straight after 'they crucified Jesus there with the criminals', they rank among the most profound ever uttered. They also take us to the very heart of Christ's message. How can anyone offer such generous forgiveness in that excruciating and humiliating situation? They have had a profound impact on Christian history. We mention two instances. The same deep sentiment, although with very different words, is expressed as Stephen is martyred: 'Lord Jesus, receive my spirit… Lord, do not hold this sin against them' (Acts 7:59–60; the juxtaposition of 'And Saul approved of their killing him' in Acts 8:1 probably indicates that they impacted and contributed towards Saul's conversion). These words also feature in Coventry Cathedral's Cross of Nails and the ministry of reconciliation which flowed out of its bombing in World War II.

However, we need to consider some of the issues they raise. First, we consider who 'they' were – for whom is Jesus seeking forgiveness? If we look backwards in the text, 'they' would be the two criminals. In support of this is the fact that one of them appears to receive forgiveness (23:39–43). These criminals were probably freedom fighters who had inadvertently made it easier for Jesus to be arrested and crucified. If we look forwards, it would be the squad of soldiers who had carried out the crucifixion: 'They cast lots to divide his clothing' (v. 34). Again, the prayer could be seen to be answered as the centurion declares Jesus innocent (23:47). Next in line would be the crowd, who 'returned home, beating their breasts' (23:48), possibly indicating repentance. Following that might be the disciples who have forsaken him, the Jewish leaders who have the main responsibility in engineering his death or Pilate and the Roman authorities. Ultimately, we can hope that we too are included.

Second, we consider whether the 'for' indicates Jesus' motive as to why they should be forgiven (for = because) or the issue for which they need to be forgiven (for = in that). On the first view, ignorance is grounds for forgiveness; on the second, it is the reason why forgiveness is necessary. The Jewish leaders should have known who Jesus was but they refused to recognise him. The Romans (especially Pilate) interrogated him and should have acknowledged what kind of leader he was.

2 'Today you will be with me in Paradise'

Luke 23:39–43

Some of the words from the cross are clearly addressed to God; others are equally clearly addressed to humans – this is the first of these. Here is the response of Jesus to the appeal and confession of one of the criminals. This criminal came to some astounding insights which lead to his confession.

First, he saw that Jesus did not deserve to be crucified: 'this man has done nothing wrong' (v. 41). Pilate had come to the same conclusion (23:14) and the centurion will confirm it (23:47). Why did Luke need the testimony of a condemned criminal to back up his defence of Jesus as innocent? In many ways, this would be at best a distraction and at worst an undermining of his case for Jesus!

The second insight was that the inscription, 'The King of the Jews', over Jesus' cross told the truth: 'Jesus, remember me when you come into your kingdom' (v. 42).

Jesus was the King of the Jews and he would be granted his kingdom. Not only is this a profound insight, but it is also an amazing confession of faith, given the circumstances. Hence, King Jesus grants this impotent petitionary his request – and more.

Jesus' statement sounds like an imperious royal declaration, beginning as it does with a sonorous 'Amen' (compare Luke 4:24; 18:17) – 'Truly, I tell you' – and it is an amazing gift: 'You will be with me in Paradise.'

Whether the 'today' goes with 'I tell you' or indicates when the promise will be fulfilled can be debated, although it seems superfluous to say, 'I tell you today'. We are probably intended to read this as indicating that Jesus will receive his kingdom very shortly and the criminal will share in it. The 'Paradise' mentioned, although coming from a Persian loan word for 'beautiful garden', probably indicates the heavenly kingdom of God (compare 2 Corinthians 12:2 and Revelation 2:7, where the same word occurs). This saying, as well as indicating the ongoing compassion and responsiveness of Jesus to human need at its most desperate, makes clear that Jesus remains confident of his own kingship and divine destination.

3 'Here is your son... here is your mother'

John 19:23–27

This word might seem so ordinary, given the Jewish context. Here, a dying man fulfils his responsibility to the last to 'honour his mother' by ensuring someone else takes full responsibility for her when he can no longer do so. It is like a will – John is the recipient of part of Jesus' inheritance: his mother. Just as with the process of 'redemption', whereby a bereaved wife with no male child was given over to the man's brother so that the family line could be preserved, so here Mary is entrusted to 'the disciple whom Jesus loved', who is normally identified with the disciple John. If Jesus had not made this 'last will and testament' statement, presumably the primary care for his mother would have passed to his natural brothers. But faith takes priority over normal family ties (see John 7:5; Mark 3:31–33).

What is somewhat more surprising is the reciprocity of Jesus saying to his mother, 'Here is your son.' Perhaps both have at their heart the concern of Jesus to mitigate against the dreadful pain of his death for his mother. Perhaps this is why his first transfer is of John to be her son. This was her deepest short-term need – someone to go on loving when Jesus is dead, as Simeon's prophecy is fulfilled: 'A sword will pierce your own soul too' (Luke 2:35). Her longer-term need for provision and protection would be met by John receiving her into his home as his mother. We should not forget, however, that Jesus' death would also be deeply painful for the disciple whom Jesus loved; making him Mary's son would ensure that he also knew a continuing love – from her. This then, appears like a very thoughtful scene from the family deathbed (see, for instance, Genesis 49:28–33, especially verse 33).

However, Jesus' death is as far away from a peaceful one as is possible and this gospel makes that clear. The previous verses contain a remarkable contrast. The soldiers who have brutally crucified Jesus act with immeasurably more thoughtfulness and respect towards his clothing: 'When the soldiers had crucified Jesus... they also took his tunic; now the tunic was seamless, woven in one piece from the top. So they said to one another, "Let us not tear it..."' (vv. 23–24).

Their respect for the tunic is in stark contrast to their disrespect for Jesus and his body. This heightens the brutality of this death scene and underlines the thoughtful compassion of Jesus both for his mother and his friend.

4 'My God, my God, why have you forsaken me?'

Mark 15:25–39; Matthew 27:33–54

If we compare this cry of dereliction, 'My God, my God, why have you forsaken me?', with the dignified silence of Socrates or the triumphant, defiant cry of 'Freedom!' by Scotland's William Wallace (at least in the film *Braveheart*), Jesus does not appear much of a hero. But appearances can be deceptive.

These words are the opening line of Psalm 22. It is worth noting that these words are recorded for us in Hebrew or, as C.F.D. Moule puts it, 'Hebrew-tinged Aramaic' (*Cambridge Greek New Testament Commentary*, 1959, p. 458). But not only Hebrew; they are also translated into Greek originally and, for us, English. This strongly suggests that they were the words Jesus uttered, in spite of the historical, pastoral and theological problems that this attribution generates. How are we to read these words – as the total cry or part of a larger utterance?

If they are the total cry, then either they offer us a sense of the absolute despair (and even disillusionment) of Jesus – his trust in God has been destroyed, he never anticipated God would allow this to happen – or we see them as the outward recognition of the consequence of Jesus being our sin-bearer: the necessary consequence of the atonement – taking the Trinity to breaking point. In support of this is the context: first, that Jesus is taunted by the onlookers, chief priests and scribes as well as his fellow sufferers (compare Isaiah 53:3–4); second, there is the atmospheric description 'When it was noon, darkness came over the whole land until three in the afternoon' (Mark 15:33). At the time when it should have been brightest, for three whole hours intense darkness enveloped the whole land, signifying the world enveloped by sin all focusing on Jesus.

The other way of understanding his cry is to note that, taken as a whole, the psalm has a different message. While the psalm is about the intensity of feeling separation from God, it ends on a note of deep trust. Often a short passage of scripture is quoted in the New Testament to indicate that a much larger passage is to be in mind. In this case, without diminishing the pain or indeed the reality of separation from God, this quotation points forward to the resurrection and indicates that Jesus died trusting his Father.

Perhaps we are meant to live in this land of mystery and uncertainty as we marvel at the Son's obedience, even to death.

5 'I am thirsty'... 'It is finished'

It is frequently noted that the words 'It is finished' contain an ambiguity. On the one hand, they could be John's equivalent to Luke's 'he breathed his last' – so they would mean, 'At last it is now all over, my whole life's work is done.' It could (but not necessarily) then imply the same sense of utter failure and disillusionment as 'My God, my God, why have you forsaken me?': 'This is how my whole life of ministry and service has ended – in total failure as my death underlines – why haven't you, God, intervened as I expected?'

Equally, it can have a very positive meaning: 'It is completed': 'The reason I came into this world to fulfil my Father's intentions have now been faithfully and completely carried out. There is no longer anything that can divert, thwart or derail my mission. The prince of this world is condemned!' It has also been pointed out that this word was used in financial transactions to indicate that a bill had been settled in full. So it is understood to indicate that Jesus has paid the complete price for the world's sin, along the lines of, 'The Lamb of God who takes away the sin of the world' (1:29). The account is settled in full.

It is less frequently noted that the preceding words, 'I am thirsty', are also ambiguous. On the surface, they express Jesus' physical condition of desperate thirst. This is how they are interpreted by the bystanders, the unspecified 'they' of John's account. Using this interpretation, the words are related to Psalm 69:21. But as Jesus and this gospel repeatedly refer to his forthcoming death as a return to his Father (see, for example, 13:1; 14:2, 12; 16:17) and the cross as his 'glorification' (12:23, 27–32), it makes sense to understand this saying rather differently. We know from Mark that Jesus' words were not always understood correctly. 'In order to fulfil the scripture' could equally well refer to Psalm 42. As with Psalm 22, Psalm 42 moves from despair and rejection to a profound expression of hope. It contains the words, 'As with a deadly wound in my body, my adversaries taunt me, while they say to me continually, "Where is your God?"' (42:10). Significantly, near the beginning it reads, 'My soul thirsts for God, for the living God. When shall I come and behold the face of God?' (42:2).

If this psalm is the scripture referred to, then the final cry, 'It is finished', provides the answer: 'The moment of vindication is complete. *Now* I will behold God's face.'

6 'Father, into your hands I commend my spirit'

Luke 23:44–49

Luke allows us to share in one last prayer from the lips of Jesus, one more insight into the reality and integrity of his faith under the most extreme conditions. It was not so long ago that we overheard Jesus in prayer to his Father, 'Father, if you are willing, remove this cup from me; yet, not my will but yours be done' (Luke 22:42).

This cup, the anticipated death by crucifixion, was also the cup of God's wrath and judgement against his chosen people in their disobedience. This cup of judgement Jesus would be called on to bear, leading to his sense of total rejection and separation from his Father.

These words from the cross recall a prayer that was frequently used by Jews as they prepared for sleep at the end of their day of toil. It comes from Psalm 31:5. Just as the words 'the day thou gavest, Lord, is ended' can refer to a whole life as well as a day, so it is in this psalm. This context would give to this prayer a sense of deep tranquillity and trust. This is underlined by Jesus' inserting 'Father' before his quotation. This was his unique signature to prayer. Luke's claim that the words were uttered as a 'loud cry' also presents them as an act of courageous commitment.

Many of the words of Psalm 31 express confidence in God's dependability, protection and action to vindicate the falsely accused. The final verses are the most insightful: 'I had said in my alarm, "I am driven far from your sight." But you heard my supplications when I cried out to you for help' (31:22). While this verse affirms the psalmist's (and Jesus') sense of ultimate vindication, the final one probably appealed to the disciples as they waited on the Lord: 'Be strong, and let your heart take courage' (31:24). This echoes the threefold appeal to Joshua on the death of Moses (Joshua 1:6–7, 9).

Whether or not all this is in the mind of the dying Jesus we cannot tell, but that it brought comfort and sense to the disciples afterwards is difficult to deny.

Guidelines

- We have noted that several of these words from the cross are capable of ambiguous, if not contradictory, meanings. Reflect on both options and consider when each might have something profound to say to our human condition. Consider whether we need to decide which is historically the more feasible in each case. Might it be that in extremis both can have coexisted in the heart of Jesus?

- Make a list of people who are in very challenging situations, including terminal illness or bereavement. Reflect on these words from the cross and pray for them in the light of these words.

- Consider the following responses to each day's reading:

  - Day 1 – These words remind us of both the need for and assurance of total forgiveness. Jesus remains the intercessor who pleads for us.

  - Day 2 – This assurance is one that all of us will need to hear at least once in our lives as we face the issue of our own death.

  - Day 3 – As we marvel at the Son's obedience, even to death, seek to live in this land of mystery and uncertainty.

  - Day 4 – Through the eyes of this gospel, experience the compassion and generosity of the king, even as he dies.

  - Day 5 – Allow these words to challenge you about your priorities.

  - Day 6 – Seek courage and strength for the challenges you may face.

Jesus and the way to the cross

Nigel G. Wright

One of the greatest of Jesus' parables is that of the son who forsook his father's house, wasted all he had and yet in time came to his senses and returned home with a penitent heart to his father (Luke 15:11–32). The willingness of that father to receive his son back, even running to meet him when he espied him from afar, is arguably the finest picture of the gracious mercy of God that we have in the whole of the New Testament. Yet outstanding as this picture certainly is, and bold as it is to say it, as a dramatisation of the Christian gospel it is radically incomplete. Missing is the understanding that the father is not content to live without his alienated child but must discover a way of seeking the lost, of beating a path into the very pigsty in which the son is living out his degraded existence and there restoring him.

In the Christian perspective, such a saving action is known as 'incarnation', and the life of Jesus might well be understood as a journey into the far country by means of which the Son of God comes 'to seek and to save the lost' (Luke 19:10). Salvation comes from the Lord, not from ourselves. Implicit in such a statement is the conviction that Christ's coming is also God's coming, since God alone can save; and so we are taken into the mysterious but marvellous territory of the holy Trinity. The drama narrated to us by scripture is that God was in Christ reconciling the world to God's own self (2 Corinthians 5:19) and that this gracious action involved not only living the life that we have failed to live but dying the death that is common to us all, doing so both with us and for us. Here is the core of Christian belief, the crucial moment in the story of salvation, the turning point that has changed the world.

So full of meaning are these moments that we rightly revisit them frequently, not least in Holy Communion. The season of Lent prepares us carefully for the days in which we particularly recollect them. It is also appropriate that once more we journey with Jesus to the cross and consider its meaning both for him and ourselves.

Unless otherwise stated, Bible quotations are taken from the New International Version (Anglicised).

1 Be careful what you ask for

Mark 10:35–45; Isaiah 42:1–4

Jesus' disciples never cease to amaze us. Not only are they persistently slow to grasp the true nature of the one they are following, but they frequently come out with questions, such as that of James and John, that can only be described as 'inappropriate'. In our reading from Mark, they are in the company of the servant of the Lord who sets them the supreme example of humility, and yet they exhibit naked ambition, the desire of both of them to know position, power and prestige in the coming kingdom. Jesus is surprisingly slow to rebuke them, but in the company of the other disciples ('indignant', no doubt, because they wanted the same), Jesus shows them the better way that finds greatness in servanthood. Precisely this way was leading him to Jerusalem and his encounter with destiny.

Jesus' way to 'glory' lies through drinking the cup of suffering and being baptised with the waters of death (Mark 10:38). He asks whether James and John can share this and foolishly they believe they can. In the event, they and their comrades would forsake Jesus when it came to the crunch. They are deluded – about themselves, as we can be. Yet, surprisingly once more, Jesus does not rebuke them. Rather, he tells them that they will indeed share in his cup and baptism. How can this be?

James and John can be forgiven for not having read the book of Hebrews with its clear emphasis on the unique and once-for-all nature of Christ's sacrifice (7:26–28). They can also be forgiven for not knowing the words, 'There was no other good enough/To pay the price of sin,/He only could unlock the gate of heaven/And let us in' (Cecil Frances Alexander, 1848). Neither book nor hymn yet existed. But surely there is a distinction here to which we must hold. It is that there is something about the cross that can only be true of Jesus, and yet there is something about the cross that must be true for us all. Our Lenten reflections that follow will explore both these truths.

A favourite and moving hymn for many of us is Isaac Watts' 'When I survey the wondrous cross'. A surveyor looks at buildings or landscapes from many aspects in order to explore their dimensions. Grasping the height, length and breadth of the cross of Christ demands much from us, but enriches us beyond measure.

2 The unique sacrifice

Jesus the Messiah has done something like no one else. His whole life can be understood as an act of self-humbling in order to offer himself in life and death as a sacrifice on our behalf. In seeking and saving the lost, he has first come to us, since to find something lost it is necessary to go to where it is. He has embraced our fallen condition as though it were his own. He has even tasted the bitterness and forsakenness of death. What was first signified in his baptism at the beginning of his ministry is to be finished in the 'baptism' of his death. Christian faith has unerringly grasped that we are all in need of salvation and are unable to save ourselves: we need a Saviour to come to our aid.

As we have seen, Jesus himself understood that he had come as a servant 'to give his life as a ransom for many' (Mark 10:45). A ransom is a price paid to set captives or prisoners free. From this derives the idea of 'redemption' and of Christ as the 'redeemer'. His identity as the Son of Man and Son of God qualifies him to act on our behalf in purchasing human salvation. He sets us free, we who are outwardly captive to powers beyond ourselves and inwardly enslaved to our own fallen natures. The whole of his life effects such a conversion and, in this, his dying for us is the furthest point to which he goes.

God cared for Israel, the people of the ancient covenant, by redeeming them out of captivity and giving them the law and circumcision to mark them out. God also provided for them a tabernacle (and later a temple), a priesthood and a sacrificial system. Through these, sins could be atoned for, their pollution cleansed and peace restored. The presence of God with the people could thus be sustained. And yet these provisions were but preparation for the concentration of God's saving work in the coming of the redeemer, the true high priest, Jesus Christ, whose once-for-all-time sacrifice of his own self (Hebrews 10:12) makes atonement not for Israel alone but for all the world (1 John 2:2). Our whole trust should be in him and in his unique life and sacrifice.

3 Pleading for mercy

Luke 18:9–14; Psalm 51

The reading from Luke exposes the folly of trusting in our own righteousness before God. Those most convinced they have achieved it are in fact the furthest away. Those who seek mercy are infinitely nearer. The tax collector's words, 'God, have mercy on me', translate literally as, 'God be propitiated to me.' The tax collector realised that he was the object of God's displeasure. He needed to sue for mercy. If we ourselves do not know this, we have understood very little about ourselves or about God.

Yet the word 'propitiate' and its cognates (as for instance in Romans 3:25 and 1 John 2:2, though variously translated) are for some the cause of embarrassment. Surely God does not need to be 'appeased'? Cannot God simply forgive, like the father in the parable, without first requiring some kind of compensation? Is the cross about God being reconciled to us or us reconciled to God?

I am inclined to agree with these hesitations and to believe that God has eternally reconciled himself to his erring, sinning children. The cross is not necessary for God, but it most certainly is for us. It is God's gracious provision for us in love. It reveals that at great cost our creator wills our reconciliation and seeks it. Indeed, this is the place, like the 'mercy seat', or place of atonement, in the temple, referred to 27 times in the Old Testament (e.g. Exodus 25:17; Leviticus 16:11–14), where we come to find grace to help in time of need. God has provided it. There is no salvation without our cry to God to have mercy. And even this is inadequate. Even at our most sincere, we are yet not sincere enough.

What makes this place one of atonement is what Christ has done for us here. Having endured the judgement of utter estrangement from the Father that we have imposed upon ourselves, he has nonetheless transformed it. He has acknowledged the death we deserve while at the same time offering to the Father a life of obedience unto death, and he has done this for us. Christ has borne the sin of many and made intercession for sinners (Isaiah 53:12). He has made the cross a plea for mercy: 'Father, forgive them, for they do not know what they are doing' (Luke 23:34).

4 Christ's cross and ours

Matthew 16:21–28; Isaiah 53:7–12

Through the cross Christ has opened up a unique pathway to the Father. In time, James and John would come to see this. Yet to our surprise, in responding to their misguided question we saw earlier, Jesus assures them that they can indeed share his final cup and baptism. The cross therefore has other dimensions to it. In its uniqueness, it is the object of our faith – Christ has died for us – but it is also something we are called to imitate, a pattern of life that all may share. Jesus himself suggested this when he called his disciples to take up their cross and follow him.

The most obvious immediate meaning is that the disciples were called to embrace martyrdom. As a matter of history, many of them did so, including James, whose relatively early death in AD44 by the sword at the hands of Herod Agrippa is recorded in Acts 12:2. Although his death was not redemptive, as was that of Jesus, it was like Jesus' death in being for a cause, a witness to the kingdom of God, an obedience unto death. It involved drinking the cup of suffering and being swallowed by the waters of death. Yet what counts is that it involved radical self-giving, a life of self-denial, a giving away of one's own life in order both to give life and gain it. Martyrdom or not, this is the pattern of life we have learnt from Jesus and whose challenge we are called to embrace.

At this point, we should observe a degree of perspective. When set against the ordinary and somewhat modest lives most of us lead, heroic thoughts of martyrdom could appear somewhat delusional (though there are still thousands of Christians who really do pay this price). Perhaps we could think of it like this: the extent to which any of us learns to overcome our tendencies towards selfishness and self-interest and practise how to give ourselves away to others – to that extent we begin to live lives that make a difference. Let it not matter that we only get there in part; to get there in the least measure makes the world a better place and points to the kingdom of peace that is still to come. We live after the example Jesus has given.

5 Breaking the cycle

This passage form 1 Peter specifically indicates that Christ is our example. It does so within a passage that enjoins upon believers the need to break the vicious cycle of recrimination rather than perpetuate it. In this sense, the cross of Christ should be seen as an act absorbing hostility and abuse rather than returning it in kind. He did not retaliate, he did not threaten, but instead he 'bore our sins in his body on the cross'. If Christ is the one who uniquely reveals God to us, then behind the cross we must also see the heart of God. If humans are God's most problematic creatures, then God has been absorbing their hostility since first they became capable of rebelling. What is amazing is that this God has borne with us and has not abandoned us.

There are those who criticise this whole way of thinking. Does it not reduce the oppressed to passivity? Does it not legitimise victimhood? Does it not minimise proper resistance to abuse? Certainly the way of the cross could be distorted into something like this, but quite wrongly so. It is rather an affirmation that ultimately the way of love will triumph over hatred, and the meek will inherit the earth. We can trust God to make sure that sin and evil will be overcome – the resurrection is the guarantee of this. In the meantime, we can take the risk of not becoming evil ourselves when confronted with evil. Like Jesus, we can with God's help absorb wrongdoing and return good for evil, trusting in God to ensure that right and truth will prevail. This is a revolutionary doctrine. It is a profoundly Christian insight.

At the heart of the human problem is our desire to strike back when we are struck, to retaliate and seek revenge when we are hurt, robbed, defrauded or oppressed. To seek justice is one thing; to seek revenge is quite another. Jesus put a stop to it; he interrupted the vicious cycle and in so doing he turned the apparent defeat of the cross into a significant victory, a turning point in the affairs of humanity. Here is a dimension of the cross that can be true for all. Were we to follow it, what a difference it might make!

6 How the light gets in

Job 38:1–11; 42:1–6; John 12:20–33

The singer-songwriter Leonard Cohen sadly died in 2016. He is well-known for the song 'Hallelujah', loved by many who may not understand what the word means. Cohen had the feel of a mystic and some of his lyrics require much thought, evoking the instinct they contain a deep meaning even though we cannot grasp it. One such is, 'There is a crack in everything, that's how the light gets in.' I take it to mean that everything contains imperfection, yet imperfection can become a place of enlightenment as an oyster's irritant grain of sand might become a pearl.

We are certainly not in a perfect world, nor do we live perfect lives. In fact, most of our lives could accurately be described as broken. Human societies certainly are and, whatever nature will one day become, in the present it too has its cracks. It is an enduring mystery, and for some an insuperable barrier to belief, why a good and loving creator should have called into being a world that is vulnerable to so many cracks. That this has been a puzzle for so many and so long is indicated in the book of Job, a superb masterpiece of literature and reflection, which wrestles with it for 42 chapters. Yet even with such massive intellectual effort, the book of Job fails to deliver us with an answer. Or at least, it tells us that the answer is hidden in the wisdom of God, before which we can only bow in humility.

The cross of Christ indicates that in him God has entered the world at its most cracked. God has embraced the darkness of creation's suffering and this presence changes it. It creates the possibility that even the worst might be taken by God in such a way as to use it for good. It is emphatically not that evil is anything other than evil, but it is a declaration that by the alchemy of divine grace even the cracks may become places where the light gets in. Paradoxically, John's gospel sees the cross as the place where Christ is not so much humiliated as glorified. He is lifted up in crucifixion, but even more so lifted up in glory, and the resurrection proclaims it. This is why we and so many are drawn to him.

Guidelines

One way to summarise the reflections we have shared is through the idea of 'participation'. It is in God's participation through Christ in our life and death that (in a manner that passes our full understanding) God has absorbed and overcome our human hostility and alienation. An ancient Christian saying has it that 'what has not been assumed has not been healed'; in other words, it was necessary for God to assume our full human condition in order for restoration to take place. Having gone to the uttermost point, Christ is able to 'save to the uttermost' (Hebrews 7:25, KJV) those who come to God through him. This is because, although he shared our life and death, he did not share our sin (Hebrews 4:15). Our response to this is to trust in what Christ has done for us, to lean all our weight upon it and make it the ground of our faith and hope.

It should be clear from this that belief in Christ is far from being a merely mental assent. Instead, it is an orientation of our whole lives towards him which brings about a transformation. Faith and works are inseparable. If Christ has participated in the pattern of our lives, it is in order that we may share in his, becoming 'like him in his death' (Philippians 3:10). Cross and resurrection are events in history, but they also create a dynamic by which we may die to ourselves and live to God.

How can we fill this out? By being people who do not seek revenge. By resolving to overcome evil with good so far as this rests upon us. By recognising that sometimes for the sake of goodness we will be taken advantage of. By determining to be givers more than takers. By praying that our tragedies as well as our triumphs might be used for the glory of God and the benefit of others. By living at peace with others and promoting peace wherever we can. By being prepared to be different in not following the pattern of this world. By living according to a higher wisdom. In short, by following Jesus on the way to the cross.

FURTHER READING

Dietrich Bonhoeffer, *The Cost of Discipleship* (SCM Press, 1959).

Peter J. Morden, *The Message of Discipleship: Authentic followers of Jesus in today's world* (IVP, 2018).

John R.W. Stott, *The Cross of Christ* (IVP, 2006).

Nigel G. Wright, *Jesus Christ – The Alpha and Omega* (BRF, 2010).

Easter Day in the gospels

Graham Dow

These six studies are from the accounts in the four gospels of the events of Easter Day. Each conveys momentous truths. They reflect the thinking of four different Christian communities. Yet all four accounts announce that it was the first day of the week. This means that, in parallel with the original creation as described in Genesis 1, the early Christian communities clearly saw the resurrection of Jesus as God's new creation, his breathtaking creative act. A new order on earth has begun; God's wonderful redemptive purposes for sinful humanity have burst into the world.

Jesus reminds the disciples that 'these are my words that I spoke to you while I was still with you – that everything written about me in the law of Moses, the prophets, and the psalms must be fulfilled' (Luke 24:44). Jewish belief held to the hope that in the end time there would be a resurrection of the righteous with the establishment of the kingdom of God on earth (John 11:24). However, the truth that Jesus was raised forced that hope to be adjusted: the end time had clearly begun. So Jesus is now alive but hidden. Until his 'appearing' (Greek: *parousia*), the disciples are simply assured of his invisible presence (Matthew 28:20) while the coming of the kingdom on earth unfolds.

The gospel accounts of Easter Day were written between 30 and 60 years after the events. Written in four quite different locations, it is not surprising that each account indicates that community's reflection on the events and its priorities. Each account has its own message, written with the overall purpose of the gospel in mind.

For Matthew, the resurrection is the redemption of the whole created order and the launch pad for the making of disciples worldwide. For Luke, describing in his two volumes how the work of Jesus continues through his church, the Easter message is about believing the facts that Jesus really is risen and about how to know him now. John's account of the resurrection brings to a climax his emphasis on Jesus being revealed as individuals come to believe in him and his charge to take abundant life from God to the world

(John 20:21). Mark's resurrection account, the first to be written, is by far the most stark. It repeats the gospel themes of astonishment and fear. A longer ending may have been lost.

Unless otherwise stated, Bible quotations are from the New Revised Standard Version (Anglicised).

1 God's great new creation

Matthew 28:1–15

Matthew signifies the in-breaking of God's new order on earth with an earthquake and terrified guards. An angel appears like lightning, rolls back the stone and sits on it. It is a highly stylised account, but we should not assume that this is an exaggeration of what happened. There was an earthquake when Jesus died (27:51–52). This is a theophany, a God-appearing; it is resurrection on a cosmic scale, for in Jesus 'all things in heaven and on earth were created' (Colossians 1:16).

Matthew's Easter Day account is the most joy-filled and upbeat: 'They left the tomb quickly with fear and great joy, and ran to tell his disciples' (v. 8). Both women had been looking on at a distance at the cross (27:56). They had come to the tomb as mourners; they left as believers. There is all the difference in the world between our story and God's. We must learn to set aside our pessimistic stories and seek to believe God's always hope-filled story.

Angels appear 300 times in scripture and cannot be written out. They appear at significant moments of God's action. After the theophany, the narrative becomes more matter of fact: 'Come, see the place where he lay… He has been raised from the dead… Go to Galilee.'

Suddenly (*idou*, 'behold', v. 9) there was a mighty earthquake; suddenly (*idou*) Jesus met them, and said, 'Hail!' (*chairete*, v. 9). He is physical and they grab his feet. 'Do not be afraid' (said twice), 'go.' Three times in chapter 28 we hear the word 'go': 'go quickly and tell his disciples' (v. 7, the angel); 'go and tell my brothers to go to Galilee; there they will see me' (v. 10, Jesus); 'go therefore and make disciples of all the nations' (v. 19, Jesus).

'Suddenly', 'don't be afraid', 'go'; there is a clear rhythm, and Jesus now calls his disciples his 'brothers'. All believers, as brothers and sisters, are united with him.

It is God's brilliance that he created these events in history. For devious motives, people will make up other explanations, but there is no other (v. 11–15). Christian faith is based on facts, not just ideas.

We are to take this upbeat message all over the world. Put away fear; be filled with joy; go. Jesus is alive and with us 'always to the end of the age' (28:20). New creation is well under way and will be until the end of time.

2 How do we know Jesus today?

Luke 24:1–32

The women who saw where Jesus was laid come back to the tomb at dawn to anoint the body, according to the law. For them, Jesus is dead. They find the stone rolled away and no body in the tomb; they are perplexed. Two men in dazzling clothes appear and the women are terrified. But the angels give the women God's story: 'Why do you look for the living among the dead? He is not here, but has risen. Remember how he told you, while he was still in Galilee, that the Son of Man must be handed over to sinners, and be crucified, and on the third day rise again' (vv. 6–7).

The women remember; they tell the apostles, who do not believe them. So God deliberately chooses to overturn the rejection of women's testimony. Peter heads for the tomb, sees the linen cloths by themselves and is amazed. As Richard Bauckham argues, this sort of eyewitness feature indicates reliable oral tradition.

With many questions still unanswered, there follows one of the most beautiful stories in the Bible. Later that Easter Day, two disciples walking home to Emmaus are discussing the things that have happened. To discuss is good. Yet they also are perplexed: Jesus 'was a prophet mighty in deed and word before God and all the people... We had hoped that he was the one to redeem Israel' (vv. 19, 21).

Taking the initiative, as always, Jesus comes unrecognised alongside them. He upbraids them, and, by implication, all the apostles, as foolish and slow of heart to believe what was there in the prophets. He interprets for them all the things about himself in the scriptures. How we would love to have heard that discourse! It makes the hearts of the two disciples burn within them (v. 32). We come to know Jesus as he opens the scriptures to us. If we genuinely seek Jesus, let us pray that he interprets his word to us. Only he can form God's story in us.

They invite him to stay. When 'he took bread, blessed and broke it... their eyes were opened, and they recognised him' (vv 30–31). Jesus vanishes, because now he is to be known by faith not by sight.

How slow of heart are we to believe, or how ready? The story indicates that Jesus opens our eyes to know him today through scripture interpreted by him, through the celebration of his death in Holy Communion, and through our asking him to share our lives.

3 Receiving understanding, then becoming witnesses

Luke 24:33–49

The two disciples return immediately to Jerusalem and share their story with the eleven apostles and their companions (v. 33). Again, Jesus takes the initiative and suddenly appears among them. He speaks, 'Peace be with you' (v. 36); we then read, 'They were startled and terrified, and thought that they were seeing a ghost' (v. 37).

Luke's narrative continues to address the difficulties people were facing in believing that Jesus was raised. Did the disciples just see some kind of ghost? Jesus challenges them: 'Why are you frightened, and why do doubts arise in your hearts?' (v. 38). He invites them to see and touch his hands and feet – those parts showing his wounds. 'A ghost does not have flesh and bones as you see that I have' (v. 39). For the final reassurance that it really is him, he asks for food and eats a piece of fish (vv. 41–43).

To support the certainty that the body of Jesus has indeed been raised by God and not stolen, Luke presents four arguments: the angels' claim that Jesus had foretold this, the linen cloths placed by themselves, the power of Jesus to interpret the scriptures to us and Jesus' sudden appearance, showing the wounds in his flesh and his capacity to eat. A scientist, John Polkinghorne, calls this a 'phase change' in Jesus' body, rather like the change from water to steam. His resurrected body, changed by the Spirit, is the mark of this new creation. It marks the arrival of God's completely new order, his kingdom on earth. The spiritual realm now greatly affects everything in the material realm. Mighty works, signs of the kingdom of God in the material creation, are to be expected by believers.

Then, just as he did for the disciples walking to Emmaus, Jesus opens the minds of the gathered disciples to understand the scriptures: 'Everything written about me... must be fulfilled... It is written, that the Messiah is to suffer and to rise from the dead on the third day' (vv. 44, 46). God's story is that the apostles, far from being confused and afraid, will now be sent by Jesus to proclaim from the scriptures repentance, accompanied with God's total forgiveness of sins. They will be witnesses of his death and resurrection to all nations; they will be 'clothed with power from on high' (v. 49). So it must be for us.

4 Jesus' relationship to the Father is also for us

John 20:1–17

John begins his account of Easter Day with a single woman, Mary Magdalene. Her desperation is obvious: 'They have taken the Lord out of the tomb, and we do not know where they have laid him' (v. 2). She just wants to be close to the dead body of Jesus.

When she breaks the news to Peter and 'the beloved disciple', they run to the tomb. Peter enters the tomb and sees the linen wrappings and the cloth that was on Jesus' head rolled up in a separate place. The 'beloved disciple' (John?) then enters; he grasps the divine story and believes. His faith is contrasted with Peter, who is yet to believe. The same pro-John comparison is made elsewhere in the gospel, reflecting a community that struggles with Peter's leadership position in the church.

On Mary's return to the tomb, two angels are present where the head and the feet of the body had been, as if to emphasise that it isn't there. 'Why are you weeping?' is the start of God's story; Mary repeats her gloomy narrative (v. 13).

Jesus appears, repeats the angels' question and adds, 'For whom are you looking?' (v. 15). Searching for the elusive Jesus is another major Johannine theme. Only Jesus can reveal himself; he responds to Mary's desperation. Thinking he is the gardener, Mary repeats for the third time her sad story; she clearly wants to find the body and take it away with her. Like the good shepherd with his sheep (10:3), Jesus calls her by name, 'Mary'; she turns round and recognises him, saying, 'Rabbouni', teacher (v. 16).

Mary is not to hold him physically; she has to learn to know him by faith.

'Go to my brothers and say to them, "I am ascending to my Father and your Father, to my God and your God"' (v. 17). This clumsy wording indicates both that she fully shares Jesus' relationship with his Father, God, but also that his relationship with his Father, and ours, are of a different order. It is in this personal relationship that we experience the true life of God (20:31)

The agreements in the four gospel accounts are striking: the first day of the week, the stone removed, the presence of angels, the wrappings still there, the headcloth folded and placed separately (contrast Lazarus in John 11:44), Jesus appearing, the disciples called brothers and the need to understand the scriptures.

5 Not by sight but by faith

John 20:18–29

Mary tells the disciples that she has 'seen the Lord' (v. 18). The woman's testimony is again the problem: when evening comes, the disciples, still unbelieving and afraid, are huddled together in fear behind locked doors (v. 19).

Taking the initiative, Jesus comes and stands in their midst. His positive story begins with 'Peace be with you' (v. 19). 'Peace', *shalom* in Hebrew, means 'complete harmony', harmony at every level. It is God's most fundamental blessing and is repeated (v. 21). Peace is what the angels announced on earth (Luke 2:14). Jesus imparted it to his disciples in the upper room (John 14:27). In a tempestuous world, believers in Jesus are to show the gift of peace they have received from God.

Jesus confirms that he is still the Word made flesh (1:14), showing them his wounds. There is a masterly understatement: 'the disciples rejoiced when they saw the Lord' (v. 20). Did they only half-believe?

The gospel in which Jesus offers life to the world reaches its climax in the heartbeat of the new order: 'As the Father has sent me, so I send you' (v. 21). With direct continuity, we are to bring God's life to the world and do the works Jesus did. As in the first creation (Genesis 2:7), so the breath of the Spirit gives the life power (v. 22). As Jesus' witnesses (15:26–27), the disciples are to have the forgiving and retaining of sins at the heart of their ministry. When accountability to God matters, the forgiveness of our sins and resulting peace belong together.

John has wrestled throughout his gospel with reasons people give for not believing. This culminates with Thomas, whose pessimism is noted earlier in the gospel. His unbelief is characterised in two ways: he refuses to believe the testimony of trustworthy friends, and he stubbornly declares his terms for believing, that is, the sight of Jesus' wounds. If that was arrogance, at least he gets two things right. First, he hangs in with his friends and is with them a week later. Second, when Jesus in great mercy comes and meets his terms for belief, he surrenders humbly and completely with the wonderfully definitive confession, 'My Lord and my God!' (v. 28).

What a climax! This may be the original end of the gospel: Jesus declares blessing on those who believe without seeing him (v. 29), that is, believing the testimony of this whole gospel, surrendering and so finding the life of God himself (v. 31).

6 Astonishment and fear

Mark 16:1–8

Astonishment is a thread running all through Mark's gospel. As he tells the dramatic story of Jesus Christ, the Son of God (1:1), peppered with words like 'immediately', there is a constant element of surprise. And so it is on Easter Day.

It is all about the women. They come with spices, expecting to anoint the body, but the body has gone. Ah, yes! A woman has already anointed Jesus for burial at Bethany at the start of Holy Week (14:8). They worry about getting the very large stone moved, but they find it has already been moved along its groove. As they enter the tomb, they find a young man dressed in white and they are 'alarmed' (v. 5). 'Do not be alarmed,' he says, rehearsing God's story with them. 'He has been raised; he is not here. Look, there is the place they laid him' (v. 6).

The man continues, 'Go, tell his disciples and Peter that he is going ahead of you to Galilee; there you will see him, just as he told you' (v. 7). Peter is named because of his denial of Christ. He is not to be disowned; he is reinstated. If, as many believe, this gospel reflects Peter's eyewitness testimony, then it reflects his humility in allowing his story to be told so fully. It is important for others to see us as fellow stumbling pilgrims.

The women 'fled from the tomb, for terror and amazement [*ekstasis*] had seized them; they said nothing to anyone, for they were afraid [*ephobounto gar*]' (v. 8). A related word for astonishment is used at the healing of the paralysed man (2:12) and of Jairus' daughter (5:42); and fear is challenged by Jesus (4:40; 6:50). The remarkable events of Jesus Christ, the Son of God, continually arouse both astonishment and fear.

While the astonishment in this chapter repeats a constant theme, it is still very surprising that the assured text ends with the women in fear and unable to spread the news. Bishop Tom Wright is convinced that the earliest copies of the gospel were mutilated. But, taking it as it is, the challenge is first to let ourselves be astonished at these amazing God events, but then also to face up to our fears and deal with them. Fears block our freedom to spread the message that Jesus is alive, and they create an impoverished church. It is God's story we must tenaciously hold on to.

Guidelines

Some questions for reflection:

- What stands out for you about the events of Easter Day? If you were writing God's version of the story, what would it say?

- How do you think our over-familiarity with the accounts diminishes our sense of wonder at the new creation God has brought about?

- In your experience, what are the common stumbling blocks to believing that Jesus physically rose from the dead? How can we persuade people that this question is relevant today?

- How did Jesus reveal himself to you? Does that experience have any parallels with Easter Day?

- How do we guard ourselves from being 'slow of heart to believe'?

- In what way do our fears affect the freedom with which we share our faith that Jesus is alive?

FURTHER READING
Richard Bauckham, *Jesus and the Eyewitnesses* (Eerdmans, 2006).
N.T. Wright, *The Resurrection of the Son of God* (SPCK, 2003).
Tom Wright, *Matthew for Everyone, part 2* (SPCK, 2002).
Tom Wright, *Mark for Everyone* (SPCK, 2001).
Tom Wright, *Luke for Everyone* (SPCK, 2001).
Tom Wright, *John for Everyone, part 2* (SPCK, 2002).

Jeremiah 25—52

Pauline Hoggarth

If you began to explore the story of Jeremiah with *Guidelines* last year, you'll be aware that 'Jeremiah doesn't provide us with an orderly narrative'! Most commentators tend to use words like 'complicated' and 'difficult' about this extraordinary text. Robert Carroll, reflecting on the interpretational challenges of a book that is rich in metaphors and ambiguities, quotes Maimonides: 'Teach your tongue to say I don't know' (Carroll, p. 85). For all its obscurities, though, Jeremiah has continued down the years to call people to brave and radical obedience to God. Dietrich Bonhoeffer identified his lonely vocation in fascist Germany with that of Jeremiah; Martin Luther King summarised the prophet's message for his contemporaries: 'The worst disservice that we as individuals or churches can do is to become sponsors and supporters of the status quo.'

Chapter 25 is approximately the midpoint of the book. Verses 1–14 seem to act as a summary and closure of the first half: Jeremiah's faithful and persistent proclamation of God's word over some 20 years has been characterised by a call to the people of Judah to turn back to the Lord in repentance. His message reflects the covenant theology of the Deuteronomy scroll, rediscovered in the temple ruins around 622BC, the 18th year of King Josiah's reign, four or five years into Jeremiah's ministry (2 Chronicles 34:14). 'Yet you did not listen to me…' (v. 7): verses 8–14 describe the catastrophic consequences of Judah's rejection of God's word – invasion, ruin, exile in Babylon. Surprisingly and shockingly, God identifies the invading Babylonian king as 'my servant' (v. 9); the Lord's sovereignty in history extends far beyond Israel to the Gentile world and includes a Gentile judgement on his people.

The texts that lie ahead in our readings include some of Jeremiah's most familiar and hope-filled words, light for our path as Christians living in exile conditions today.

Unless otherwise stated, biblical quotations are from the New Revised Standard Version (Anglicised). Author references are to works in the 'Further reading' list.

1 Whose truth?

Jeremiah 26

Claims about what truth is and who speaks truth are at the heart of Jeremiah 26, a sequence understood by a number of scholars as an expansion of the events recorded in chapter 7, Jeremiah's 'temple sermon'. Chapter 7 provides a detailed account of what the prophet proclaimed, but nothing about the response of his hearers. In chapter 26, we have the reverse: a brief account of a message that Jeremiah claims as God's word to his people (vv. 2–6; 12) and an extended description of the furious responses of religious and political leaders and the public, culminating in death threats and a hastily arranged trial (vv. 8–11).

The focus of public outrage is Jeremiah's unambiguous declaration that unless the people of Judah recognise their failure to live by God's standards and turn back to him, Jerusalem and its temple will be destroyed and abandoned like the ancient Shiloh worship centre (7:12–15; Psalm 78:59–66). This is the truth that Jeremiah believes to be rooted in God's covenant word (vv. 12, 15). It is in direct opposition to the claim of the Jerusalem royal-religious establishment, that the prophet's verdict on city and temple is false and he deserves the death sentence (vv. 9, 11). Perhaps to underline the risk Jeremiah takes, his story is juxtaposed with the grim narrative of the prophet Uriah (vv. 20–23), extradited from Egypt and murdered by King Jehoiakim for proclaiming the same message as Jeremiah.

Maybe Jeremiah's courageous willingness to die for the truth he proclaims and his careful warning against even more severe consequences (vv. 14–15) begin to prick consciences. Surprising voices join the debate. For unspecified reasons, some civic leaders and the public begin to acknowledge the source of Jeremiah's claims (v. 16). A group of senior citizens recalls a precedent from a century before, in the time of King Hezekiah and the prophet Micah (vv. 17–19). Some commentators suggest that this subversive group, the 'elders of the land', probably came from outside the Jerusalem establishment elite, maybe not even living in the capital. They were not the recognised power brokers. Like Micah, observing urban corruption from rural Moresheth (Micah 1:1; 3:12), like Jeremiah in Anathoth, it seems they were among those voices from the margins that play such a crucial part in God's story, telling the truth against all the odds. Micah's message had not fallen on deaf ears. Hezekiah had repented; the temple and city still stood intact. Now King Jehoiakim and his people face the same choices. Without repentance, 'great disaster' stares them in the face (v. 19).

2 Shock tactics

At the time of the Falklands/Malvinas war in 1982, a courageous pastor in Buenos Aires preached a series of sermons on texts from the Old Testament prophets. With the grief of a Jeremiah, he denounced the violence and corruption of the military regime of the time and acknowledged the conflict as both judgement and opportunity for repentance. But he also warned the United Kingdom, whom he understood as the Lord's permitted means of judgement, against complacency: like Babylon (vv. 6–7), the UK also faced God's scrutiny and judgement.

Chapters 27 and 28 work together in a similar way to chapters 7 and 26 as message and response, though they do not follow chapter 26 chronologically. They are set at the start of the reign of Zedekiah, Nebuchadnezzar's vassal king in Jerusalem, whom we last encountered pleading with Jeremiah, in the face of imminent Babylonian invasion, to put in a good word with God on his behalf (21:1–2). By now, the first wave of that invasion has taken place (597BC) and the first exiles have left Judah.

We imagine the scene as Jeremiah, responding to God's directions, constructs the awkward and uncomfortable leather and wood yoke and struggles into it. Word gets around as people speculate about what the prophet is going to say this time and what the yoke might mean. Nothing prepares them for the shock of hearing God's call to *submit* to the domination of Babylon, to be prepared to serve Nebuchadnezzar (v. 8) and reject the voices calling them to rebel (v. 9). The message is reiterated specifically for King Zedekiah and reinforced: *submission* to the Babylonian yoke is the only way to survive (vv. 12–13). It is also directed via their ambassadors to the rulers of surrounding nations who found themselves dominated by the superpower of the time – verse 3 might hint that these nations were conspiring with Zedekiah against Babylon.

Jeremiah's scandalous message, especially his challenge to the smooth-tongued prophets of peace (v. 16), provoked a defiant response. Chapter

28 details how the opposition prophet Hananiah smashed Jeremiah's symbolic yoke and was in turn warned that the wooden yoke would become iron, 'because you have spoken rebellion against the Lord' (28:16).

We are left with many questions at the close of these chapters and their apparent message that 'the God of the Bible effectively tilts the international process' (Brueggemann, p. 243). As we view our world today, to what extent do we understand *all* nations as morally accountable to God and their flourishing or decline as in some way linked to God's values? Isaiah 47 and Romans 2:1–16 are texts that may help our reflections.

3 Experiencing exile

The Lord's original calling to Jeremiah had two contrasting emphases. His work would be 'to destroy and to overthrow' but also 'to build and to plant' (1:10). As well as the painful message of judgement, there was to be a pastoral dimension to his ministry, clearly demonstrated in his remarkable letter sent to the Jews who had been living in exile in Babylon since 597BC. 2 Kings 24:8–17 provides an account of the brief and corrupt reign of Jehoiachin/Jeconiah, the Babylonian siege of Jerusalem and the captivity and exile of a major part of the population of Judah. Nebuchadnezzar seems to have targeted for exile an elite group of Jews (Daniel was among them – see Daniel 1:1–7), alongside royalty, the military and talented artisans.

The false prophet Hananiah had confidently proclaimed a brief exile of two years (28:3, 11). Now a crucial part of Jeremiah's pastoral task is to prepare his people in Babylon to cope with the truth, a painful, long-term understanding of these turbulent events – an exile of 70 years (v. 10). Painful, yes, but also strangely realistic and hopeful: the letter opens with a surprising call to stability, productivity, relationship, intercession for the well-being of the alien community among whom the exiles find themselves and rejection of the rose-tinted lies peddled by false prophets (vv. 5–9). On the exiles' commitment to 'seek the welfare [*shalom*] of the city' where they experience exile and to 'pray to the Lord on its behalf' depend God's glorious promises of return and restoration, 'a future with hope' (v. 11). Exile, it seems, for all its pain, is full of possibility. Jeremiah's letter rejects self-pity and proclaims, 'The only opportunity you will have to live by faith is in the circumstances you are provided this very day' (Peterson, pp. 152–53). Exiles such as Daniel bear witness to the possibilities of faithfulness to God in limited circumstances (Daniel 1:8; 2:17–18, etc.).

Jeremiah's hope-filled interpretation of the situation was not without cost to him. He was challenged by the Jerusalem-based faction, who refused to listen to God's messengers (vv. 16–19) and also by the exiles, attracted by lying prophets. Three of them are named – Ahab and Zedekiah (vv. 21–23) and Shemaiah (vv. 24–32), whose communication to the priests in Jerusalem quotes Jeremiah's own letter (v. 28) and mocks him for 'playing the prophet'.

4 All things new...

Jeremiah 31:31–34; 32:6–25

At the time of writing these reflections, events in the world seem to be dominated by a sense of weariness, anxiety and anger. Hope is in short supply. It is hard for followers of Jesus to trust the God who reveals himself as the Alpha and the Omega, who is 'making all things new' (Revelation 21:5–7). Jeremiah's bracing, compassionate letter to the exiles introduces a section of prophecies whose theme is overwhelmingly hopeful (chapters 30—33). The God who 'has pledged to work a newness precisely where there is no evidence of such newness on the horizon' (Brueggemann, p. 267) provides a word to which we may submit our hopelessness. These chapters are often referred to as the 'Book of Consolation'; their fulcrum is the reminder of the Lord's unchanging love and faithfulness (31:3) and the 'new covenant' he promises to establish with his people (31:31).

This is the only specific Old Testament reference to the new covenant – though the prophets often declare that God will do something new (for example, Ezekiel 36:26; Isaiah 42:9). Some commentators warn against reading this promise of the new covenant primarily or only in its New Testament context (Hebrews 10:16–17). God's pledge is addressed out of the blue to the people of Judah and Israel because of his desire for relationship with them (31:32). This covenant is to be an inwardly motivated relationship, not dependent on religious expertise, wholly rooted in the Lord's grace that is beyond belief or deserving (31:33–34). Maybe we see something of the outworking of this heart-relationship with the Lord in exiles like Daniel and Nehemiah and in Jeremiah himself, for whom God is all in all.

The intriguing account in chapter 32 of Jeremiah's purchase of a field in his home town of Anathoth illustrates something of what an all-in-all relationship with God may mean. Trust in the hope of newness demanded practical action. In human terms, this transaction was lunacy: with the Babylonians about to invade (32:2), it made no sense for Jeremiah to buy his cousin's land to preserve the family inheritance (32:8). The meticulous details underline how deliberate a decision Jeremiah takes (32:9–14). We witness bold commitment on the outside to what the Lord has said (32:14–15); on the inside is turmoil that Jeremiah turns into urgent prayer to the God of steadfast love (*hesed*) for whom nothing is too hard – or is it (32:17–25)?

5 Message to a prisoner

Jeremiah 33

It takes courage to act on the basis of hope. God's immediate response to Jeremiah's honest prayer had been immensely encouraging: 'I am the Lord… is anything too hard for me?' (32:27). That crazy purchase of land would be one of many future transactions, made by people whose hearts had been transformed by the Lord (32:40–44).

But God hasn't finished with providing encouragement. True, the closing section of the Book of Consolation opens rather unhopefully with Jeremiah still under arrest on the orders of King Zedekiah, Nebuchadnezzar's puppet in Jerusalem (v. 1, compare 32:2–3). But the message that God addresses to his prophet is deeply hopeful, shaped as a series of words or oracles of promise. The first (vv. 2–9) urges the prophet to look beyond the despair and horror of the destruction around him to future healing, rebuilding, security and joy from the hands of the creator God who unfailingly listens and responds. That vision is expanded in verses 10–11 into the gentle, reassuring details of normal human life – laughter, celebration, song and worship. The third image (vv. 12–13) of the restoration of pasture land and of shepherds 'resting their flocks' and counting them reverses the disorder, violence and lostness of invasion and exile. Next (vv. 14–16) comes an almost exact repetition of the promise found in 23:5–6 of a future ruler who will practise justice and righteousness: 'Royal Israel will act in ways that make new life possible' (Brueggemann, p. 318). The final three words of promise all speak of different continuities – of priesthood (v. 18), king (v. 17) and community (v. 22) – reaching back to the foundation of God's creation covenant and the Davidic covenant that followed (vv. 20, 25).

Prophecy has many layers of interpretation. Some of this magnificent vision granted to Jeremiah was fulfilled when the Jewish people returned from exile in Babylon to rebuild Jerusalem (Ezra 1:1–4). But we know that more occupation and subjection followed. The Jewish people would be dominated by other world powers. From the perspective of the New Testament, we understand these prophecies to be fulfilled in Jesus, the branch growing from Jesse's root (v. 15; see also Romans 15:12).

'I… will have mercy upon them' (v. 26) is the closing promise of the Book of Consolation. 'It is precisely in exile, when all seems lost, that mercy comes to the fore as God's primal way with Israel' (Brueggemann, p. 322) – with his people then and now.

6 Keeping faith?

Jeremiah 34:8–22; 35:1–19

God's name, often written as LORD in English Bibles, is the translation of the Hebrew YHWH, revealed and interpreted to Moses as 'I am who I am' (Exodus 3:14). The name expresses the Lord's utterly faithful character. The editorial process of these two chapters seems deliberately to juxtapose two episodes that illustrate people's unfaithful and faithful responses to the fundamental character of God. There is no chronological order here – the story of the faithless double dealing with slaves takes place in the reign of Zedekiah, last king of Judah (34:8) and that of Rechabite integrity some ten years earlier in the times of Jehoiakim (35:1). Both follow a further message of judgement on king Zedekiah (34:1–7) and, taken together, provide an urgent message about the nature of fidelity and the price to be paid for infidelity.

This is the only information we have about Zedekiah's command to his people to set free their Hebrew slaves. The law of Moses made humane provision for Jews who became indebted and had to sell themselves as slaves; they must be liberated and their debts cancelled after a set period (Exodus 21:1–6; Deuteronomy 15:1–11). Was the king's 'covenant' a sudden, panicked reaction to avert God's promised judgement? And what prompted the people's reversal (v. 11)? Maybe Jerusalem's economists pointed out the cost of cancelled debt, and self-interest won the day against any concern for compassionate Torah provisions. God cares about economic exploitation. 'Therefore' (v. 17) introduces the appalling consequences for people and king. The previous invasion (598BC) will be followed by a second (587BC).

The narrative now moves back ten years to an odd encounter between Jeremiah and an unusual group of people. Under normal conditions, the Rechabites were nomadic, tent-living people, metal-workers whose countercultural way of life dated back to the times of Jehu, over two centuries previously. They have moved into Jerusalem only because of the invasion (v. 11). Apparently under God's instructions, Jeremiah sets up a test of the Rechabites' integrity (v. 5), which they pass with flying colours (vv. 18–19).

The story is not about the merits of being teetotal or nomadic. It's about an alternative society that chooses to listen and live responsively (vv. 6–9), in sharp contrast to the carelessness and disobedience of the majority around them.

Guidelines

- 'Those voices from the margins that play such a crucial part in God's story' (p. 125). Take time to reflect on some of the Bible's other 'marginal' people and their place in God's story – for example, the Hebrew midwives Shiphrah and Puah (Exodus 1:15–21), Naaman's wife's servant girl (2 Kings 5:1–5) and the first witnesses to the resurrection (Luke 24:1–11). What other names would you include? To what extent do you think that the church today takes notice of its marginal voices?

- How do you find yourself relating to God's dual calling of Jeremiah to 'destroy and to overthrow' and 'to build and to plant' (1:10)? Is this dual calling true of all Christian leadership? What has been your own experience of these vocations?

- 'This is the work of the exile – not the discovery of a new gospel, or a new Christ, or a new Bible, as some more liberal thinkers have suggested, but the rediscovery of the original genius of the teaching of Jesus and the missional practice of the earliest Christians, all lived out boldly on the soil of a post-Christian empire' (Frost, p. 26). What common ground do you discern between Michael Frost's description of Christians' experience of 'exile' today and Jeremiah's 'letter to the exiles' in chapter 29?

- As you reflect on the contrasting accounts of debt-bound people re-enslaved (34:8–22) and the countercultural lifestyle of the Rechabites (35:1–19), which do you find to be a greater challenge to the life of the church today, and why?

1 A dangerous text

Jeremiah 36

Chapters 36–45 of Jeremiah appear to be organised as a narrative unit, written in the third person, mostly in prose and mostly concerned with events in the prophet's life. Chronologically, this section predates the chapters we have just been reading, taking us back to 605BC, early on in the reign of Jehoiakim (v. 1). This was a time of massive political turmoil in the region; the Babylonian armies advanced relentlessly and the Judean king was trapped in a power struggle between Egypt and Babylon. The history of these times is recorded in 2 Kings 23:29—25:30.

We have already met the scribe Baruch in a later episode, acting on behalf of Jeremiah in the purchase of land (32:11–17). But before that, Jeremiah had called on Baruch in response to God's instruction to provide a complete written record of what he, the Lord, had been saying to Judah, Israel and the surrounding nations since he first called Jeremiah to his prophetic task in the days of Josiah (vv. 2, 4). At this point, the prophet himself is no longer free to proclaim God's word in the temple (v. 5); there is a probable connection here to Jeremiah's outspoken proclamation of God's judgement in the 'temple sermon' of chapter 7 and the fallout from it detailed in chapter 26. He had escaped execution, but his movements were now strictly controlled by the authorities.

One of the most intriguing aspects of this chapter is its description of the mysterious process by which the word of God may become written scripture. The initiative is God's; the words are God's, not Jeremiah's (vv. 1–2). The process of dictation and recording results in a text of human words whose impact, it seems, even God cannot guarantee – 'It may be…' (v. 3). A range of audiences listen to the reading of his written message – the people gathered in the temple (v. 10), the temple officials (vv. 11–15) and finally the king and his officers (v. 21).

The encounter between the highest human authority in the land and the authority of God's word could not be more dramatic. The king cuts and burns the scroll deliberately and systematically (v. 23), utterly unmoved by Baruch's reading and challenging its truthfulness (v. 29). What courage that reading must have demanded of Jeremiah's scribe!

'Take another scroll…' (vv. 28): that second, expanded text (v. 32) points to the determination of the Lord never to leave his people without knowledge of his character and his will.

2 Prophetic work, private life

Jeremiah 37:1–21; 38:1–6

Zedekiah was the third of Josiah's sons, a puppet king in the hands of Nebuchadnezzar, who had even changed his name (2 Kings 24:17). His reign was notoriously corrupt and offensive to the Lord (2 Kings 24:19–20), his outstanding characteristic a refusal to listen to God's word addressed to him through Jeremiah (37:2). Incongruously, he combines that rejection with a plea to Jeremiah to address a special prayer to the Lord (37:3). This seems to be the second of Zedekiah's requests to the prophet for special pleading with God – the first, for Nebuchadnezzar's siege to be lifted (21:1–2); now, because of the Egyptian threat and the resulting lifting of the Chaldean siege, for some unspecified rescue. In both cases, the Lord's response is uncompromising (21:5): the Chaldeans will not go away and Jerusalem will burn (37:10).

What follows is a fascinating and touching insight into how Jeremiah's personal life interacted with his prophetic calling. In the midst of threats and turmoil, both inside and outside the walls of Jerusalem, Jeremiah has private concerns. Commentators differ on whether the property mentioned here is the same land he had taken the risk of buying from his cousin Hanamel in Anathoth (chapter 32). Anathoth was certainly in the land of Benjamin (37:12). The withdrawal of the besieging army offers the prophet an opportunity to leave the city to deal with the matter. But Jeremiah is no longer an anonymous private citizen; he is known for promoting submission to Babylon and he has encouraged surrender to the enemy (21:8–10). Maybe there was a curfew. The reaction of Irijah the sentinel is understandable (37:13). And like the rest of the Jerusalem power-brokers, 'Irijah would not listen' (37:14).

A brutal beating and a first period of imprisonment follow for Jeremiah – no one must be allowed to question the corporate lie promoted by those in power (37:19; 38:4), though King Zedekiah clearly has his own private doubts. What irony in his anxious question to the prophet (37:17)! His initial reasonable treatment of Jeremiah is quickly swept away by the astute bullies who surround him. For them, the only good Jeremiah was a dead one (38:4–5). Like Pontius Pilate some six centuries later, Zedekiah washes his hands of a troublesome prophet and consigns him to an agonisingly slow death.

3 A good man

Jeremiah 38:7–28

The Bible record gives us occasional glimpses of ordinary people who courageously practised God's values of justice and mercy in the midst of dangerous political realities. During the reign of Ahab and Jezebel, a minor courtier called Obadiah who 'revered the Lord greatly' rescued, hid and fed the Lord's prophets who were under threat from the queen (1 Kings 18:1–4). For Ebed-melech, an Ethiopian official in Zedekiah's court, God's concerns also had priority and propelled him to brave and compassionate action. The story is a curious mixture of bare narrative bones and unexpectedly rich detail that hints that Baruch the scribe might have been an eyewitness of at least some of what happened!

We know that Jeremiah had influential friends in Jerusalem – they had already rescued and protected him several times (26:17–19, 24; 36:19). Maybe Ebed-melech had links to this group. No explanation of his intervention is offered at this point in the narrative and we are left to speculate about the directness with which the courtier informs the king about Jeremiah's situation and boldly accuses his officials (v. 9). Shortly before, Zedekiah had yielded to Jeremiah's enemies (v. 5). Now he yields to Jeremiah's friend (v. 10). He seems to have been a man who responded without reflection to the latest demand. The lively details of the rescue itself (vv. 11–13) were surely watched by Baruch, who seems impressed and moved by Ebed-melech's humanity and practical kindness (those rags to pad Jeremiah's armpits!).

Ebed-melech's brave intervention makes possible a final encounter between prophet and king (vv. 14–26). The relationship has changed – Zedekiah no longer rejects Jeremiah's analysis of the situation. He candidly admits his fears of his own people who are allying themselves with Babylon (v. 19), perhaps aware at last that he has left it too late to take Jeremiah's/God's advice and submit to the enemy (vv. 20–23). The encounter ends with the king demanding a lie from Jeremiah and the prophet colluding with the king, with the result that those who exercise power will no longer hear

God's word (v. 27). Did Jeremiah agree to the king's proposal so as to ensure his own survival to speak God's word? This is one of the most poignant moments in the Jeremiah story and confronts us with what it may mean to seek to be God's person in humanly impossible circumstances.

4 Jerusalem falls

Jeremiah 39

Scripture provides us with three accounts of the siege and eventual capture of Jerusalem, probably in January 588BC (2 Kings 25:1–12 and Jeremiah 52:4–16 are the other two). The siege lasted some 18 months (vv. 1–2) and left the population entirely without food (2 Kings 25:3). Reports from Yemen in the present day remind me of the horrors of famine conditions and the toll they take on the most vulnerable.

As in the most effective media reporting, the story of Jerusalem's fall is told through its impact on individuals – on Zedekiah, the last Davidic king (vv. 4–8), on the prophet Jeremiah (vv. 11–14) and on the Ethiopian courtier who had saved Jeremiah's life (vv. 15–18).

The grim account of the atrocities perpetrated on Zedekiah, his family and the Judean elite tends to overshadow some less violent aspects of the Babylonian occupation. The burning and destruction of dwellings seems to have been selective, not wholesale (v. 8), there is no evidence that the temple was damaged and the most impoverished members of society even benefited from the invaders' redistribution of property (v. 10). These details are repeated in all three biblical accounts. But the people, especially the elite, suffered. Zedekiah's terrified flight into the desert didn't save him from his Chaldean pursuers, who caught him near Jericho and handed him over to Nebuchadnezzar's torturers at his base in Syria (v. 5). Given Zedekiah's perfidy, he was fortunate to end his life in exile, blinded, but in a kind of peace (34:1–5; but compare 52:11).

And Jeremiah? The Babylonian soldiers discover him in Zedekiah's guard house (v. 14). Had word reached Nebuchadnezzar of Jeremiah's prophecies urging cooperation with the invaders? The narrative offers no explanation for the privileged treatment he receives. He is handed over to the son of a family who had a history of supporting him (see 26:24) and becomes an example of what he himself had so faithfully proclaimed – the need to submit in order to live.

The closing episode of this chapter takes place when Jeremiah is still under arrest (v. 15). In all the chaos of siege and invasion, God's word comes again to his prophet in a message that epitomises Jeremiah's original calling to tear down and build up (1:10). Ebed-melech will witness the destruction of the city but will himself be saved. God has not forgotten the man who showed mercy to his prophet and whose outstanding characteristic was his trust in the Lord (v. 18).

5   Still faithful?

Jeremiah 40:1–6; 42:1–17; 43:1–7

God's words to his people of warning and judgement, of healing and hope, have been vindicated. The royal-religious elite in Jerusalem who defied Babylon and toyed with an Egyptian alliance are gone, having been slaughtered or exiled. There is deep irony in the theological analysis of events from the Babylonian captain in charge of Jeremiah (40:2–3). Scripture records other 'outsiders' with a surprising insight into God's ways; the centurion at the cross is one example (Mark 15:39).

The respectful treatment that Nebuchadnezzar ordered for Jeremiah includes complete freedom of movement: 'See, the whole land is before you' (40:4). This second, expanded account of Jeremiah's situation (compare 39:11–14) details a food allowance and gift, which must surely have identified him even more clearly as a collaborator: 'The Jeremiah tradition never finishes sorting out the vexed challenge that faithfulness to God seems to some to be treason to royal Jerusalem' (Brueggemann, p. 376).

Gedaliah, the Jewish leader with whom Jeremiah chose to take refuge, is now appointed governor of conquered Judah (40:7). He seems to have been a wise and honourable man whose doctrine of 'remain and flourish' was similar to Jeremiah's. But his governorship is brief – he is murdered by Ishmael, a rogue member of the royal family (41:1–3). In a situation of growing chaos, Johanan, a Gedaliah supporter (see 40:13–16), seeks out Jeremiah with the familiar plea to reveal God's will – but now only for the 'remnant' (42:2).

Once again, it is an unwelcome message that the Lord demands from his prophet. It's no longer 'submit to Babylon' but 'remain in this land' (42:10) and don't be tempted to move to Egypt (42:15). It's met with complete rejection and accusations against Baruch (43:2–3).

The most sobering aspect of this episode is the apparent seriousness with which Johanan and the 'remnant' request God's direction through Jeremiah (42:2–3) and their response to the prophet's warning that they are going to hear *all* the truth (42:4). The people commit themselves to obedience (42:5). So why was God's compassionate and hopeful message so brutally rejected (43:2)? Had Johanan and his supporters already decided on their future in Egypt (41:16–17)? Was Jeremiah suspect, too close to Babylon? The episode closes on a note of anger and grief: 'They came into the land of Egypt, for they did not obey the voice of the Lord' (43:7). Among them came Jeremiah and Baruch.

6 Thus far…

'It is the supreme irony of Jeremiah's life that it ended in Egypt, the place that represented everything that he abhorred' (Peterson, p. 194). At various times in the life of God's people, Egypt had offered a seductive alternative to the demanding business of living by faith in God (Genesis 12:10–20; Exodus 16:1–3; 1 Kings 9:16). Jeremiah now witnessed his people taking up Egyptian idolatry, the libations and offerings to the queen of heaven, and warned them that God's righteous anger would overtake them and their host nation. Egypt was no escape route (44:29–30). The only word of mercy is directed to the faithful but despairing scribe Baruch (45:2–5).

The six chapters that follow the brief note about Baruch contain prophetic words addressed to 'the nations'. They follow the ominous note of 'disaster upon all flesh' (45:5). God's original appointment of Jeremiah had been to pronounce God's word 'over nations and over kingdoms' (1:10). We have already heard God's word of judgement – and sometimes hope – directed to the nations of the known world (25:15–38). Now Egypt, Philistia, Moab, Ammon, Edom, Damascus, Kedar, Elam and Babylon are in turn considered in the light of God's global sovereignty. The prophetic word against Babylon is the most extensive of these oracles (50:1—51:58). It also receives special instructions for delivery to its intended audience, detailed in verses 59–64, and almost certainly an editorial addition to bring Jeremiah's record to a close.

Nebuchadnezzar, king of Babylon, died in 562BC, his kingdom still in one piece. It was only under his son, Amel-Marduk, that Babylonian power started to crumble and was finally eclipsed at the hands of the Persian empire under Cyrus in 539BC. Jeremiah's Babylon oracle looks ahead to these events; the closing section (vv. 47–58) declares Babylon's defeat and destruction.

Babylon has been a constant theme throughout Jeremiah: the dominant world power of the time and God's instrument of judgement on his rebellious people. Jeremiah proclaimed that obedience to God required submission to this power. The oracle against Babylon reminds us that God's chosen instruments of judgement are themselves judged and that 'the dynamic of public history is indeed a theological dynamic, and not a matter of power politics' (Brueggemann, p. 463).

Guidelines

- 'Nothing could be farther from the truth than the facile belief that God only manifests himself in progress... Real spiritual progress can only be achieved through catastrophe and suffering, reaching new levels after the profound catharsis which accompanies major upheavals' (W.F. Albright, quoted in Peterson, p.192). As you look back over the events of Jeremiah's life, the message he proclaimed, its impact and lack of impact and the evidence of his inner life, what aspects of his ministry and character do you find most important to consider and learn from for church and society today? Where do you discern 'real spiritual progress' and how would you account for it?

- 'Prophets are people who, because of their roots in the theological tradition and because of some emancipatory experience in their own life, refuse to accept the definitions of reality that are imposed upon us by the socio-economic political power structure. In ancient Israel, the prophets refused to accept the royal-priestly ideology of the Jerusalem establishment, and they kept saying that the radicality of the Torah was more definitive than what was going on in Jerusalem' (Walter Brueggemann, in an interview with *Image Journal*). How might these readings in Jeremiah help us to examine again some of the apparent 'givens' in our society and even in church practice, and reimagine them in the light of Jesus' radical good news? Are there practical ways in which these reimagined situations might become realities?

- For meditation and prayer: 'O come, let us worship and bow down, let us kneel before the Lord, our Maker! For he is our God, and we are the people of his pasture, and the sheep of his hand. O that today you would listen to his voice!' (Psalm 95:6–7).

FURTHER READING

Walter Brueggemann, *A Commentary on Jeremiah: Exile and homecoming* (Eerdmans 1998).

Robert P. Carroll, *Jeremiah: A commentary* (SCM, 1986).

Michael Frost, *Exiles: Living missionally in a post-Christian culture* (Hendrickson Publishers, 2006).

Tremper Longman III, *Jeremiah, Lamentations* (Hendrickson Publishers, 2008).

Eugene H. Peterson, *Run with the Horses: The quest for life at its best* (InterVarsity Press, 1983). There is a revised 2009 edition.

Overleaf… Guidelines forthcoming issue | Author profile |
Recommended reading | Order and subscription forms

Guidelines forthcoming issue

HELEN PAYNTER

On first thought, it might be hard to feel confident that an ancient set of writings like the Bible can have any meaningful points of connection with the lives we live in the twenty-first century. Sure, I'm guessing that most who read this will be willing to agree with their relevance for spiritual truth: for salvation, knowledge of God, future hope, and so on. But how does the ancient world of slow travel, community orientation, and vulnerability to the natural world intersect with our busy, technology-focused, individualistic lives? Can the ancients really have anything to say that will help us to be good disciples in our own day?

Well, the contributors to the next edition of *Guidelines* certainly think so. Because, partly through the brilliance of outgoing editor David Spriggs, who commissioned these notes, but also perhaps by a glorious set of 'coincidences', in the next issue of *Guidelines* we will find a rich tapestry of reflections on how discipleship looks in the twenty-first century. Let me focus on a few of them.

The contemplative life draws some and repels others, probably based as much upon personality type as on spiritual maturity. And most of us would associate it with a withdrawal from the world, perhaps a shunning of modern conveniences. In a week of biblical reflections on the contemplative life, Paul Bradbury anchors it firmly into modern challenges. For those of us in church leadership, how do we set boundaries around our availability? How does contemplation connect with reading the world around us?

In an insightful fortnight of readings on Ecclesiastes, Peter Hatton invites us to reflect on modern arrogance and hubris. 'Any human belief in the ultimate importance of our toil and our strivings is madness and folly', he tells us. The giddy pursuit of pleasure and wealth, our frantic efforts to avert ageing and death, the folly of workaholism: these are all remarkably contemporary themes, which the sage has much to teach us about.

Another set of reflections that I'm excited to offer is from David Kerrigan, who explores the theme of mission in its gloriously fullest, most holistic expression. In relation to science, economics, social media and politics, he invites us to ask, 'How is God's rule expressed here?' And we have three other rich weeks on the theme: two from David Walker, exploring some more of the challenges that Christians and churches today face, and one from Michael Parsons, considering what the ancient practice of discipleship looks like in 2020.

But it's invidious to choose highlights. We will also have the opportunity to linger long and deeply in several biblical books. I've already mentioned Ecclesiastes; add to that Fiona Gregson on Philippians, Andy Angel on Matthew 8—10, Matt Lynch on 2 Chronicles and my own contribution on Joshua.

And then we have a wild card – not the author, who is well known to *Guidelines* regulars, but the topic. Bishop Graham Dow writes a week of thought-provoking reflections on the established church, which this dissenter finds much to approve of and agree with!

All in all, an exciting round-up, as I hope you will agree. May God bless us all as he fills the open hearts of writers and readers alike.

Why the Bible matters to me: Helen Morris

The Bible includes several images and metaphors to describe the value of God's word: more precious than gold and sweeter than honey (Psalm 19:10); sharper than a double-edged sword (Hebrews 4:12); rain that waters the earth (Isaiah 55:10); fire (Jeremiah 23:29); sustenance (Matthew 4:4); and seed (Luke 8:11). The image I've chosen to focus on is that of God's word as a light (Psalm 119:105). In context, the psalmist is referring to a light that guides the way, helping the lover of God's word to walk in right paths. Elsewhere, though, the image of 'light' is used to depict not just God's word, but God himself, most powerfully in Revelation 21, where the light of God and the lamb illuminates the new creation (Revelation 21:23).

The use of 'light' to depict both God and his word emphasises the intimate connection between the two. God is not – like a tree, an atom or a neutron star – an object that we can study. As the transcendent 'other', the creator and not creation, he is distinct from all that he has made. His nature is veiled to us unless, as he has in his grace, he makes himself known. It is at the heart of evangelical theology, and my own faith commitment, that God has made himself known through Spirit-inspired scripture. God's word is not just a light that guides the way, but a light that reveals God himself – although, as Paul puts it, we now see but dimly (1 Corinthians 13:12).

The Bible attests that God reveals himself most fully in his Son, who, as the very image of God, makes the Father known. But, before we make any false antithesis between God's revelation in his Son and his revelation in scripture, we should remind ourselves that John's first description of Jesus is the Word made flesh (John 1:14). The power of scripture's written words is their Spirit-breathed ability to point to the Word himself.

Therefore, the Bible matters to me, first and foremost, because through it I encounter God, as Father, Son and Holy Spirit. Through scripture, the triune God speaks to me, challenges me, comforts me, corrects me and reveals his character to me. The heavens proclaim the glory of God (Psalm 19:1). Yet, it is only as the Bible articulates God's nature and acts in the words of narrative, poetry, law code, song, lament, prophetic oracle, historical account, proverb, letter and apocalypse that I am able to see with some clarity. This clarity increases when I read the individual sections of scripture mindful of their context in the whole. I've found that, the more I grasp the metanarrative of scripture, how the books connect together to reveal God's plans for his creation from start to finish, the more I am struck by God's sovereign power and unfathomable love, the more inspired I am to wonder and praise, and the more equipped and enthused I am to walk by the Bible's light.

An extract from *You Are Mine*

You Are Mine
Daily Bible readings from
Ash Wednesday to Easter Day
DAVID WALKER

In the BRF Lent book for 2020, David Walker explores different aspects of human belonging through the medium of scripture and story in order to help us recognise the different ways in which we are God's beloved. And as we recognise ourselves and our own lives in the narrative of God's engagement with humanity and his creation, he gently challenges us to engage for God's sake with God's world.

I can still picture the faces of many of those who have taught me. Each in their way has influenced not only what I know but also what I value and how I behave. A sixth-form maths teacher instilled in me a desire not just to find the right answer but to get there by the most elegant and simple route. A university lecturer kindled in me a love for the most abstract of concepts. A college tutor helped me to develop confidence in myself as a public speaker. What's more, that practice of having a teacher who guides and inspires me didn't end when I knelt before a bishop to be ordained; it continued through the more experienced clergy with whom I worked in my early adult years, through to the diocesan bishop who was my first colleague after my own episcopal consecration and on to the professor who leads the group of scholars with which I do much of my theological research and reflection. To have a teacher is not to lack confidence in my own capabilities and experience, but it is to realise that I am still learning.

The title of teacher, or rabbi, is applied to Jesus a lot in the gospels. As with my own experience, it means much more than someone who imparts information. In fact, there is little suggestion that Jesus followed the widespread tradition of teaching his disciples large chunks of material that they then had to recite back to him accurately. We only have one prayer that he appears to have taught them to use. And even the Lord's Prayer itself reads more like an example or an outline around which anyone can build their own particular petitions.

Rather, the disciples accompanied Jesus from place to place as he ministered and were increasingly invited and entrusted to prepare the ground in the towns and villages he intended to visit. With greater or lesser degrees of success, during his earthly ministry and afterwards, they copied the kinds of things they had seen him doing. They took on the values that he espoused and demonstrated the love and forgiveness that lay at the heart of his teaching. Through this they became the community that began the process of converting large chunks of humanity to become his followers too.

At the heart of this lay the fact that he had never actually stopped being their teacher. Before his crucifixion, he had assured them, as recorded in John's gospel, that he would dwell within them. Matthew tells us that Jesus' final meeting with his disciples after his resurrection contained a promise to be with them until the end of the age. Jesus was true to his word. He went on being their teacher, and Christians around the world find him exercising that same role in their lives today.

A few years ago there was a fashion, especially among teenage Christians, for wearing a plastic wristband with the letters WWJD on it. The initials stood for 'What would Jesus do?' and were a simple invitation for the wearer to imagine how Christ would respond to the situation they were in before they fixed on a course of action. The fashion was treated by some with disdain.

It was alleged to be simplistic, not least by seeking to find a direct answer from Jesus to a situation that could never have occurred during his earthly ministry. Nevertheless, I believe a great truth lies at its heart. If Jesus is our teacher, and we belong with him in at relationship as his first disciples did, then like them we should seek to copy his behaviour, even if that requires an effort of imaginative prayer rather than direct observation.

Moreover, that attempt to imagine the action and reaction of Jesus in a particular situation takes place in a much wider context. The Christian who takes Christ as teacher is seeking to follow the pattern of his teaching and the example of his life, not just in response to some isolated ethical dilemma but day in and day out. Through the imitation of Christ, a discipline that goes back down the centuries, we are slowly but surely transformed into his image, just as in the ancient world the goal of many a pupil was to become ever more like their master. As we grow in the likeness of Jesus, the work of behaving as he would becomes ever more natural to us, sustained by repetition as well as by our abiding relationship with him in each present moment.

Come Lord Jesus,
and be our teacher,
as you taught the people of Israel long ago.
May we so follow your good example
that we grow ever more in your likeness,
until we take our place in heaven. Amen

To order a copy of this book, please use the order form on page 149 or visit
brfonline.org.uk.

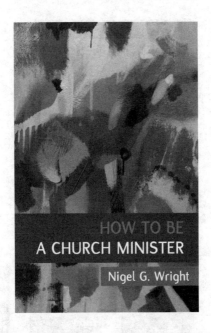

This timely book sets out what is involved in being a Christian minister – its joys and challenges, its responsibilities and privileges. It discusses the call to and the work of ministry; the breadth and nature of the task. It will enable you to understand your calling more fully and inform your practice. It will stimulate careful and biblical reflection. *How to Be a Church Minister* is relevant across a wide spectrum of church traditions, both to those already in ministry and to those contemplating the vocation. It is set to be a seminal volume on the subject.

How to Be a Church Minister
Nigel G. Wright
978 0 85746 689 1 £10.99
brfonline.org.uk

AVAILABLE NOW: **NEW HOLY HABITS** RESOURCES

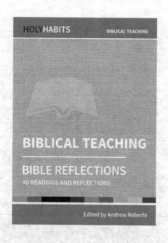

Holy Habits is an adventure in Christian discipleship. Inspired by Luke's model of church found in Acts 2:42–47, it identifies ten habits and encourages the development of a way of life formed by them.

Building on the Holy Habits resources published at the start of 2019, these Bible Reflections and Group Study materials are designed to help small groups and individuals build Holy Habits through Bible reading and group discussion questions. Easy to use, from a variety of different contributors, these booklets are the perfect addition to help your church's Holy Habits journey to thrive and flourish.

Holy Habits Bible Reflections
Edited by Andrew Roberts
£3.99

Holy Habits Group Studies
Edited by Andrew Roberts
£6.99

Available February 2020:
BREAKING BREAD | SHARING RESOURCES | SERVING |
GLADNESS AND GENEROSITY | WORSHIP

Find out more at **brfonline.org.uk/holy-habits**

In this helpful book, grounded both in personal experience and in extensive research amongst retired ministers, and rich in quotations from an eclectic range of writers, Paul Beasley-Murray explores how retirement is part of God's rhythm for our lives and provides encouragement and insights for this next stage of the journey.

Make the Most of Retirement
A guide for ministers
Paul Beasley-Murray

978 0 85746 864 2 £7.99 published February 2020
brfonline.org.uk

To order

Online: brfonline.org.uk
Telephone: +44 (0)1865 319700
Mon–Fri 9.15–17.30

Delivery times within the UK are
normally 15 working days. Prices are
correct at the time of going to press
but may change without prior notice.

Title	Price	Qty	Total
Really Useful Guides: Genesis 1—11	£5.99		
Really Useful Guides: Psalms	£6.99		
Really Useful Guides: John	£5.99		
Really Useful Guides: Colossians and Philemon	£5.99		
BRF Lent book: You Are Mine	£8.99		
How to Be a Church Minister	£10.99		
Make the Most of Retirement	£7.99		

POSTAGE AND PACKING CHARGES			
Order value	UK	Europe	Rest of world
Under £7.00	£2.00		
£7.00–£29.99	£3.00	Available on request	Available on request
£30.00 and over	FREE		

Total value of books	
Postage and packing	
Total for this order	

Please complete in BLOCK CAPITALS

Title _____ First name/initials _____ Surname_____

Address_____

_____ Postcode _____

Acc. No. _____ Telephone _____

Email_____

Method of payment

☐ Cheque (made payable to BRF) ☐ MasterCard / Visa

Card no. ☐☐☐☐ ☐☐☐☐ ☐☐☐☐ ☐☐☐☐ ☐☐☐☐ ☐☐

Expires end ☐☐ ☐☐ Security code* ☐☐☐ Last 3 digits on the reverse
of the card

Signature* _____ Date _____ /_____ /_____
*ESSENTIAL IN ORDER TO PROCESS YOUR ORDER

Please return this form to:
BRF, 15 The Chambers, Vineyard, Abingdon OX14 3FE | enquiries@brf.org.uk
To read our terms and find out about cancelling your order, please visit **brfonline.org.uk/terms**.

The Bible Reading Fellowship (BRF) is a Registered Charity (233280)

How to encourage Bible reading in your church

BRF has been helping individuals connect with the Bible for over 90 years. We want to support churches as they seek to encourage church members into regular Bible reading.

Order a Bible reading resources pack

This pack is designed to give your church the tools to publicise our Bible reading notes. It includes:

- Sample Bible reading notes for your congregation to try.
- Publicity resources, including a poster.
- A church magazine feature about Bible reading notes.

The pack is free, but we welcome a £5 donation to cover the cost of postage. If you require a pack to be sent outside the UK or require a specific number of sample Bible reading notes, please contact us for postage costs.

How to order and find out more

- Email **enquiries@brf.org.uk**
- Telephone BRF on +44 (0)1865 319700 Mon–Fri 9.15–17.30
- Write to us at BRF, 15 The Chambers, Vineyard, Abingdon OX14 3FE

Keep informed about our latest initiatives

We are continuing to develop resources to help churches encourage people into regular Bible reading, wherever they are on their journey. Join our email list at **brfonline.org.uk** to stay informed about the latest initiatives that your church could benefit from.

BRF Transforming lives and communities

BRF is a charity that is passionate about making a difference through the Christian faith. We want to see lives and communities transformed through our creative programmes and resources for individuals, churches and schools. We are doing this by resourcing:

- **Christian growth and understanding of the Bible.** Through our Bible reading notes, books, digital resources, Holy Habits, conferences and other events, we're resourcing individuals, groups and leaders in churches for their own spiritual journey and for their ministry.
- **Church outreach in the local community.** BRF is the home of two programmes that churches are embracing to great effect as they seek to engage with their local communities: Messy Church and Anna Chaplaincy.
- **Teaching Christianity in primary schools.** Our Barnabas in Schools team is working with primary-aged children and their teachers, enabling them to explore Christianity creatively and confidently within the school curriculum.
- **Children's and family ministry.** Through our Parenting for Faith programme, websites and published resources, we're working with churches and families, enabling children and adults alike to explore Christianity creatively and bring the Bible alive.

Do you share our vision?

Sales of our books and Bible reading notes cover the cost of producing them. However, our other programmes are funded primarily by donations, grants and legacies. If you share our vision, would you help us to transform even more lives and communities? Your prayers and financial support are vital for the work that we do. You could:

- support BRF's ministry with a regular donation (at **brf.org.uk/donate**);
- support us with a one-off gift (use the form on pages 153–54);
- consider leaving a gift to BRF in your will (see page 152);
- encourage your church to support BRF as part of your church's giving to home mission – perhaps focusing on a specific area of our ministry, or a particular member of our Barnabas in Schools team.
- most important of all, support BRF with your prayers.

Help us raise God-connected children and teens through a gift in your will

Aged twelve, Jesus went with his family to Jerusalem to celebrate the Feast of Passover. After the festival, the family began their journey home, but Jesus was not among them. He stayed behind 'in the temple courts, sitting among the teachers, listening to them and asking them questions' (Luke 2:46, NIV).

It's a picture that may sound familiar to some parents. Perhaps you can remember a time when you were trying to get your kids ready for school, a family meal or another engagement. There was much to do and time was slipping away, but all your kids wanted to do was ask questions about anything and everything.

As a parent, you often want to encourage your children to ask questions, spiritual or otherwise, so that they can learn and discover new things. But life must go on and those shoe laces won't tie themselves! It's a tricky predicament.

Our Parenting for Faith team understands this dichotomy. They aim to equip parents and carers to confidently parent for faith in the midst of the mundane: when ferrying the children back and forth, sitting on the bathroom floor potty-training toddlers or waving kids off on their first day of secondary school.

Through their website, an eight-session course and numerous events and training opportunities, the Parenting for Faith team are helping Christian parents raise God-connected children and teens. They're helping to raise a new generation that can bring God's love to a world in need.

Could you help this work continue by leaving a gift in your will? Even a small amount can help make a lasting difference in the lives of parents and children.

For further information about making a gift to BRF in your will, please visit **brf.org.uk/lastingdifference**, contact us at **+44 (0)1865 319700** or email giving@brf.org.uk.

Whatever you can do or give, we thank you for your support.

Pray. Give. Get involved.
brf.org.uk

SHARING OUR VISION – MAKING A GIFT

I would like to make a gift to support BRF. Please use my gift for:

☐ where it is needed most ☐ Barnabas in Schools ☐ Parenting for Faith
☐ Messy Church ☐ Anna Chaplaincy

Title	First name/initials	Surname

Address	

	Postcode

Email

Telephone

Signature	Date

giftaid it You can add an extra 25p to every £1 you give.

Please treat as Gift Aid donations all qualifying gifts of money made

☐ today, ☐ in the past four years, ☐ and in the future.

I am a UK taxpayer and understand that if I pay less Income Tax and/or Capital Gains Tax in the current tax year than the amount of Gift Aid claimed on all my donations, it is my responsibility to pay any difference.

☐ My donation does not qualify for Gift Aid.

Please notify BRF if you want to cancel this Gift Aid declaration, change your name or home address, or no longer pay sufficient tax on your income and/or capital gains.

Please complete other side of form ➡

Please return this form to:
BRF, 15 The Chambers, Vineyard, Abingdon OX14 3FE

BRF

The Bible Reading Fellowship is a Registered Charity (233280)

SHARING OUR VISION – MAKING A GIFT

Regular giving

By Direct Debit: You can set up a Direct Debit quickly and easily
at **brf.org.uk/donate**

By Standing Order: Please contact our Fundraising Administrator
+44 (0)1865 319700 | **giving@brf.org.uk**

One-off donation

Please accept my gift of:

☐ £10   ☐ £50   ☐ £100   Other £ [＿＿＿＿＿]

by (*delete as appropriate*):

☐ Cheque/Charity Voucher payable to 'BRF'

☐ MasterCard/Visa/Debit card/Charity card

Name on card

Card no. [＿＿＿＿] [＿＿＿＿] [＿＿＿＿] [＿＿＿＿]

Expires end [M M] [Y Y]   Security code* [＿＿＿]

*Last 3 digits on the reverse of the card
ESSENTIAL IN ORDER TO PROCESS YOUR PAYMENT

Signature   Date

☐ I would like to leave a gift in my will to BRF.

For more information, visit **brf.org.uk/lastingdifference**

For help or advice regarding making a gift, please contact our Fundraising
Administrator +44 (0)1865 319700

☞ Please complete other side of form
Please return this form to:
BRF, 15 The Chambers, Vineyard, Abingdon OX14 3FE

BRF

The Bible Reading Fellowship is a Registered Charity (233280)

GUIDELINES SUBSCRIPTION RATES

Please note our new subscription rates, current until 30 April 2021:

Individual subscriptions
covering 3 issues for under 5 copies, payable in advance
(including postage & packing):

	UK	Europe	Rest of world
Guidelines 1-year subscription	£17.85	£25.80	£29.70
Guidelines 3-year subscription (9 issues)	£50.85	N/A	N/A

Group subscriptions
covering 3 issues for 5 copies or more, sent to one UK address (post free):

Guidelines 1-year subscription	£14.10 per set of 3 issues p.a.

Please note that the annual billing period for group subscriptions runs from 1 May to 30 April.

Overseas group subscription rates
Available on request. Please email **enquiries@brf.org.uk**.

Copies may also be obtained from Christian bookshops:

Guidelines	£4.70 per copy

All our Bible reading notes can be ordered
online by visiting **brfonline.org.uk/collections/
subscriptions**

GUIDELINES

Guidelines is also available as
an app for Android, iPhone and iPad
brfonline.org.uk/collections/apps

GUIDELINES INDIVIDUAL SUBSCRIPTION FORM

All our Bible reading notes can be ordered online by visiting
brfonline.org.uk/collections/subscriptions

☐ I would like to take out a subscription:

Title _____ First name/initials _____ Surname _____

Address _____

_____ Postcode _____

Telephone _____ Email _____

Please send *Guidelines* beginning with the May 2020 / September 2020 / January 2021 issue (*delete as appropriate*):

(*please tick box*)	UK	Europe	Rest of world
Guidelines 1-year subscription	☐ £17.85	☐ £25.80	☐ £29.70
Guidelines 3-year subscription	☐ £50.85	N/A	N/A

Total enclosed £ _____ (cheques should be made payable to 'BRF')

Please charge my MasterCard / Visa ☐ Debit card ☐ with £ _____

Card no. ☐☐☐☐ ☐☐☐☐ ☐☐☐☐ ☐☐☐☐

Expires end ☐☐ ☐☐ Security code* ☐☐☐ Last 3 digits on the reverse of the card

Signature* _____ Date _____/_____/_____

*ESSENTIAL IN ORDER TO PROCESS YOUR PAYMENT

To set up a Direct Debit, please also complete the Direct Debit instruction on page 159 and return it to BRF with this form.

Please return this form to:
BRF, 15 The Chambers, Vineyard, Abingdon OX14 3FE

To read our terms and find out about cancelling your order, please visit **brfonline.org.uk/terms**.

The Bible Reading Fellowship (BRF) is a Registered Charity (233280)

GL0120

GUIDELINES GIFT SUBSCRIPTION FORM

☐ I would like to give a gift subscription (please provide both names and addresses):

Title .... First name/initials .... Surname ....

Address ....

.... Postcode ....

Telephone .... Email ....

Gift subscription name ....

Gift subscription address ....

.... Postcode ....

Gift message (20 words max. or include your own gift card):

....

....

Please send *Guidelines* beginning with the May 2020 / September 2020 / January 2021 issue (*delete as appropriate*):

(please tick box)	**UK**	**Europe**	**Rest of world**
Guidelines 1-year subscription	☐ £17.85	☐ £25.80	☐ £29.70
Guidelines 3-year subscription	☐ £50.85	N/A	N/A

Total enclosed £ .... (cheques should be made payable to 'BRF')

Please charge my MasterCard / Visa ☐ Debit card ☐ with £ ....

Card no. ☐☐☐☐ ☐☐☐☐ ☐☐☐☐ ☐☐☐☐

Expires end ☐☐ / ☐☐   Security code* ☐☐☐   Last 3 digits on the reverse of the card

Signature* .... Date .... /....... /.......

*ESSENTIAL IN ORDER TO PROCESS YOUR PAYMENT

To set up a Direct Debit, please also complete the Direct Debit instruction on page 159 and return it to BRF with this form.

Please return this form to:
BRF, 15 The Chambers, Vineyard, Abingdon OX14 3FE

To read our terms and find out about cancelling your order, please visit **brfonline.org.uk/terms**.

The Bible Reading Fellowship (BRF) is a Registered Charity (233280)

You can pay for your annual subscription to our Bible reading notes using Direct Debit. You need only give your bank details once, and the payment is made automatically every year until you cancel it. If you would like to pay by Direct Debit, please use the form opposite, entering your BRF account number under 'Reference number'.

You are fully covered by the Direct Debit Guarantee:

The Direct Debit Guarantee

- This Guarantee is offered by all banks and building societies that accept instructions to pay Direct Debits.
- If there are any changes to the amount, date or frequency of your Direct Debit, The Bible Reading Fellowship will notify you 10 working days in advance of your account being debited or as otherwise agreed. If you request The Bible Reading Fellowship to collect a payment, confirmation of the amount and date will be given to you at the time of the request.
- If an error is made in the payment of your Direct Debit, by The Bible Reading Fellowship or your bank or building society, you are entitled to a full and immediate refund of the amount paid from your bank or building society.
- If you receive a refund you are not entitled to, you must pay it back when The Bible Reading Fellowship asks you to.
- You can cancel a Direct Debit at any time by simply contacting your bank or building society. Written confirmation may be required. Please also notify us.

The Bible Reading Fellowship

Instruction to your bank or building society to pay by Direct Debit

Please fill in the whole form using a ballpoint pen and return it to:
BRF, 15 The Chambers, Vineyard, Abingdon OX14 3FE

Service User Number: | 5 | 5 | 8 | 2 | 2 | 9 |

Name and full postal address of your bank or building society

To: The Manager	Bank/Building Society
Address	
	Postcode

Name(s) of account holder(s)

Branch sort code

| | | - | | | - | | | |

Bank/Building Society account number

| | | | | | | | | |

Reference number

| | | | | | | | |

Instruction to your Bank/Building Society
Please pay The Bible Reading Fellowship Direct Debits from the account detailed in this instruction, subject to the safeguards assured by the Direct Debit Guarantee. I understand that this instruction may remain with The Bible Reading Fellowship and, if so, details will be passed electronically to my bank/building society.

Signature(s)

Banks and Building Societies may not accept Direct Debit instructions for some types of account.